Glorious Glouces....

With all good wishes.
Wallis Rue

FOR

CAROLE TAYLOR

Glorious Gloucestershire

by

Wallis Peel

GIETE

Copyright © Wallis Peel 2005
First published in 2005 by Giete
Loundshay Manor Cottage
Preston Bowyer
Milverton Somerset TA4 1QF
www.amolibros.com

Distributed by Gazelle Book Services Limited
Hightown, White Cross Mills, South Rd
Lancaster, England LA1 4XS

British Library Cataloguing in Publication Data
A catalogue record for this book is available from the British Library

ISBN 0-9547268-1-2

Typeset by Amolibros, Milverton, Somerset
This book production has been managed by Amolibros
Printed and bound by T J International Ltd, Padstow, Cornwall, UK

Contents

❧❧∞❧❧

About the Author

Wallis Peel is the writer of numerous published books, short stories and newspaper features. She is a long-established member of the Society of Authors.

She had the normal working-class education of her era but she hated school and left at fourteen. She spent one miserable year in offices then followed her heart's desire to work with horses. She started at the bottom of the pile and worked her way up as she gained experience and knowledge. She started writing in her late twenties then had gaps because of one thing or another but always, at the back of her mind, was the desire to write.

Glorious Gloucestershire is a collection of articles written for two Gloucestershire papers over a period of several years.

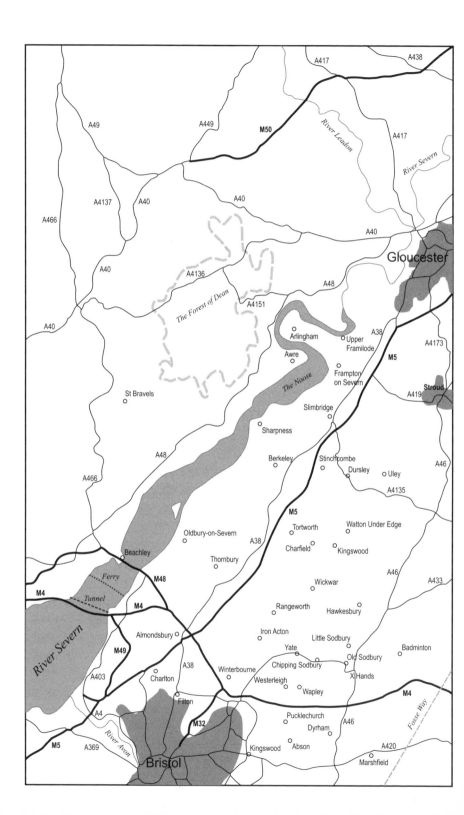

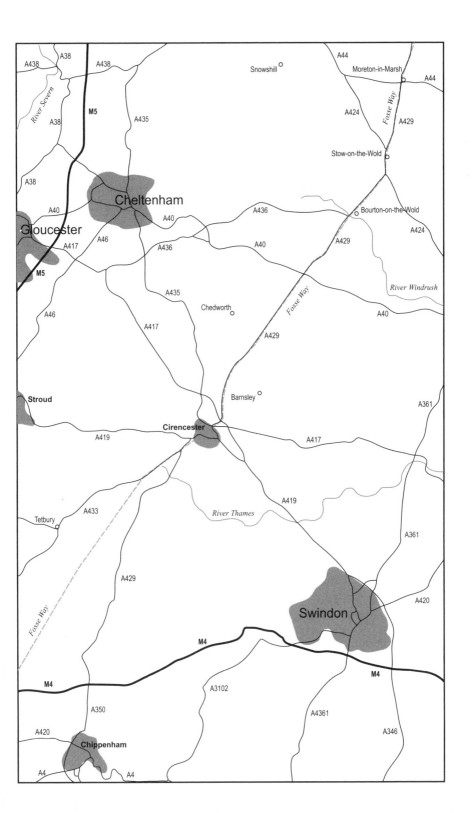

That County

❮❮❯❯

'That County' is the title of a sad poem written during World War I by a private of the Gloucesters who was a prisoner of war. It is both a lament and praise for his homeland and his County and is in T A Ryder's book a *Portrait of Gloucestershire*. As Ryder says, the soldier is describing his homeland, a County with no violent peaks or troughs; but a round and gentle, green landscape. That which all of us know today.

It was not always like this though. There were times, millions of years ago, when this land heaved with violent convulsions, when it sweated with a jungle atmosphere, then froze from bitter ice. There had been volcanoes, floods, deluges and all hell on earth which seems impossible to us today.

Thanks to the film *Jurassic Park* and then later *Walking with Dinosaurs* we almost feel familiar with such settings yet how different is that about which we think to the actuality. The Jurassic period was 193 million years ago and life was about reptiles ruling as they increased in size and variety with some even taking to the air. Birds developed their feathers so they too could fly but many of these were not the dainty singing creatures that inhabit our bird tables. Some were vicious raptors, destined to get even larger. They would become so enormous they could easily have beaten up a jumbo jet if such had existed then.

It was the next period, the Cretaceous which saw the dinosaurs take over the ruling crown. It is difficult to imagine a dinosaur on top of Uley Hill looking down at today's Dursley area for food or a mate. How did man get on among all these savage giants? He did not have to because he did not yet exist which was just as well. Primitive man was not due to appear for thousands of years and when he did, he would be called Men of the River Drift. These were the early ancestors of our County's people.

While waiting on evolution's calendar, great changes would take place that would have a significant bearing on the future of our County. The land was periodically drowned by the sea and left behind clues in shell life, found in many places. It sweltered when the climate was hot and steamy and African-type animals like elephant roamed around.

Then there would be violent convulsions, great earth movements and the climate would go from very hot to bitterly cold as the ice advanced to smother life. At the same time its heavy weight would be responsible for the contours of the land and when the ice periodically retreated, its melting would gouge out valleys, forming that which one day would be our familiar landscape.

Sometimes the seas would be shallow, at other times much deeper, laying down sludge in which deposits accumulated. At one period, from today's Tortworth to Charfield a line could have been drawn which gave the sea's level and during which the various limestones from the carboniferous ages were settling down. In the present day these would be excavated like that at Chipping Sodbury Quarry.

There were deposits of old red sandstone, now known as the Trias marls, very common around Yate. These became the source of the famous Celestine or Strontium Sulphate – a very uncommon ore but one of great industrial value even today. At one time, Yate produced ninety-five per cent of the world's demands, an extraordinary event. The workings were always surface ones, nothing but large holes in the ground and the mineral itself was clean and colourless or slightly blue or pink. A very pretty ore.

At one period, when the sea did deepen, mud and silts were deposited to form Lisa clay and a large part of the Severn Vale has this. It makes for a heavy soil but is suitable for dairy farming when the land has been properly drained.

Another very famous rock was formed during the Jurassic period, oolitic limestone, which was to become famous and prized for buildings as, once constructed, this stone blends in well with the landscape.

Some clay beds gave us the valuable Fullers Earth which was vital during the sheep rearing and clothing industry times. It has always been used for degreasing the sheep's wool before it can be washed and then spun. Very valuable to the clothiers.

Only two million years ago, in the Pleistocene age, the glaciers stormed backwards and forward and the sea levels rose and shrank but the landscape very gradually started to take on its present appearance. Ape-like creatures with some intelligence appeared who were able to make stone tools. Did they live in our County? It is possible but there was one enormous drawback. Early man needed caves in which to live, to take refuge against man-eating carnivores. A cave gave some degree of security with a fire at its entrance yet our County has never exactly had that many caves. Unlike some others. It is perhaps possible that primitive man was unenthusiastic about our area for this very reason.

Then, 10,000 years ago, a mere bagatelle in the geological calendar, the seas rose once more and this island became separated from the rest of Europe. But with a now more moderate and temperate climate, forests started to grow and man began to take over. From very primitive man to a slightly more advanced kind our ancestors were now firmly settled on this island. Bold men sailed from Europe to conquer, settle and intermarry with those already here.

The land too had established itself. As forests had been ground down by the various climates, they had rotted and made the coal belt. Colder weathers had tamped this down ever deeper. Wind and storm had shaped the hills and valleys aided and abetted by retreating glaciers.

Rivers, stream and springs were all in place. So were the rocks and ores. Man had progressed slightly and organised himself into units and tribes. His homes were nothing but pathetic huts, wattle and daub with luck. His life expectancy was incredibly short but a nucleus of proven tough tribal members would always survive to make our ancestors.

It is these people and this carefully carved landscape for which the soldier yearned from behind the barbed wire and to that which he meant with his title 'That County'.

Roman Roads

The Romans and their magnificent roads are justifiably famous even today but how and why did they come about? Gloucestershire must have delighted them. It had all they required and was especially eyed with favour where the land rose high to make the Cotswolds.

Without a doubt, the Britons would have had their own tracks, many centuries old but these any well bred, military Roman would have scorned as pathetically useless. Any trail and track would do for the Britons just as long as it went from point A to B. Bends and curves were accepted without a second thought. All the Britons wanted was a rideable path for their sure-footed ponies. A way to gallop, often in single file, to keep tribes in contact to wage internecine warfare, which they adored usually as a hobby. So long before the Romans came, the whole County was criss-crossed with trails and the Romans simply stamped their authority with enormous improvements.

The Romans were a very enlightened people and from the earliest days of their martial conquests, they realised they could never hold such a vast empire under subjugation unless they had brilliant communications. The saying arose that 'all roads lead to Rome', which was perfectly accurate.

A great number of these incredible constructions have vanished during the last 2,000 years but some do still remain. Modern roads have been laid over their foundations and, in other places, they are proudly signposted for drivers. In Gloucestershire the famous *Fosse Way* knifes through the county and is the main artery of Moreton in the Marsh. The *Akeman Street* ran from Cirencester and, slightly further north, The *Fosse* is bisected by the *Watling Street*. The *Fosse* itself runs from today's Exeter right through to Lincoln. These vitally important roads meant the Romans had absolute control over the centre of the country and also increased the importance of Gloucestershire to Rome itself.

If the Romans did have a mental blockage it was that which concerned bends and curves. They abhorred these. To any well-bred Roman, the simplest and quickest way between two points was nothing but a simple, straight line. If anything was unfortunate enough to stand in their proposed way it was simply obliterated. Only the largest of obstacles gave them pause for thought and it was always with the most extreme reluctance they would allow a diversion to occur and, even then, no curves. Just another straight road at an angle before it would join up, as soon as possible, with the original.

The fighting men of the Legions always came first so right on their heels would be the road-builders. The surveyor was the prime key and there were two types: the land surveyor, called an agrimensore, and the actual road surveyor known as the gromatici. These men, especially the latter, had to undergo the most rigorous training, usually in the army. They were equipped with very accurate instruments and worked to a high standard.

The basic instrument was known as the groma. This was something set into the ground or could be held vertically. There was a cross bar from which hung four plumb lines so constructed they hung at right angles. There was also a bracket which swivelled to allow free sight of these lines. They also had range poles, all of which gave the desired straight lines and right angles for the eye.

Unfortunately there was no fixed point for the eye which meant repeated sightings from many points and these might produce errors which, if added up, would have played havoc with the Romans' vital straight lines.

Without a portable screen these lines would only swing in the wind so sometimes shallow tubes would be used. From what we do know, Roman surveyors surprisingly lacked any optical instruments. They relied solely upon the human eye which, in turn, meant distances between stations were short, often only one or two miles.

We do not know exactly how they worked out their mathematical formulae though it is presumed Pythagoras' Theorem would have been used. Distances selected would have been multiples of three, four and five. It is thought that instruments to measure divided right angles were still unknown.

Measuring rods were used though. They even had an early-toothed wheel which drove a device in a small carriage and was called a hodometer. This dropped a stone into a bronze vessel every mile.

The Roman mile was based simply upon one thousand paces of a runner's stride of five feet, which worked out at about 1,620 yards. Naturally there were variations with the length of the feet especially on what might be called minor roads.

The main roads like the *Fosse Way* and the *Ermine Way*, both roads of Gloucestershire, as well as the famous *Watling Street*, would be measured in standard miles as far as we can work it out.

They knew all about levelling instruments which were vital for working on aqueducts but their only use in road surveying would have been for estimating the quantities of material used in embankments which, in turn, would have come from cuttings.

An embankment was called an Agger and was considered most important. To start with, the surveyor would explore the proposed route on foot. He would study the land's geology, and note the terrain as well as the types of soil and plants. Once this had all been sorted out the next vital step was to have an absolutely accurate north and south or east and west orientation. This would be marked out because on this would depend the whole accuracy of the operation and the Romans were precise and fussy.

If a river made an obstacle distances had to be calculated allowing for bridging. With a very steep and large hill they might, just, condescend to use a zigzag though this went against all Roman instincts for straightness.

An average road would have an agger and two side ditches. They were from where the spoil was taken to make the agger but they had a secondary use for drainage. Most of their roads were about thirty feet wide and rarely were pedestrians considered with pavements unless in the centre of towns.

Roman roads were built for marching Legions, wheeled traffic carrying goods and couriers with despatches from Rome. All else was simply by the by.

The road's foundations were remarkable. The Romans would dig deeply then start the foundations, bringing material from elsewhere if necessary. The ground had to be firm; the bedding must never give way and the whole thing be capable of carrying heavy traffic.

They would use wooden piles, brushwood and concrete. The top surface had to be durable and suitably cambered. At times they would use material from old iron mines like slag or clinker. Over the decades this would bed down and, with rain, the material would turn into a kind of metal strip. It is not unknown, even today, for an old, long hidden Roman road to show itself. In a violent thunderstorm the lightning would automatically find this hidden metal and race along it in a bolt of fire, burning all in its path.

In the towns the road would have a generous width sometimes of fifty-seven feet and a central carriageway of twenty-seven feet. There might even be timber kerbs at some edges. The surface could be red gravel mixed with pebbles in washed loan. Then there would be another layer of pebbles, pooled and mixed with sand. The final topping could even be concrete. Certainly the Romans built their roads to last.

The Romans scorned the Britons' ideas of bridges. They considered them pathetic affairs. They made solid, boxed bridges and, even today, nearly 2,000 years later, it is not unknown for some persons to turn up a remarkably strong affair. Their bridges might have a timber platform though sometimes it would be metalled with small stones. The uprights would be tipped with iron which, in turn, would be driven very deep into the riverbed with a pile driver.

Today we expect signposts and milestones. To start with, the Romans considered these quite unnecessary trivialities. It is thought the reason is that a main-roads' traveller would always be able to find someone to advise him. At crossroads too the Romans liked to have a shrine. One favourite goddess was Trivia or Diana of the crossroads.

The few milestones which did exist were cylindrical and might carry an official inscription of honour to the current emperor. Sometimes it might commemorate a building or the road itself.

Road maintenance was considered most important. Weeds would be cleared and verges scythed, ditches kept clean. These tasks would fall upon the local community whether it liked it or not.

The Roman roads were a marvel of their times, and so many have disappeared only through neglect after the Legions were pulled out. Once their 400 years' occupation of this island ended, the invaders who then came could not be bothered with roads.

At times the Romano-British would put the road out of commission deliberately. Without the Legions, and knowing Saxons and then Danes itched to invade, the indigenous inhabitants realised the acute danger of the roads' excellent communications so many of them were hidden and Nature simply did the rest.

It is a remarkable tribute to the Romans that some of their roads do exist in this twenty-first century with heavy truckers thundering down them. How many though are there still hidden from our eyes?

Our Wonderful Barriers

Our boundaries are unusual and some so ancient they have to pre-date the Romans especially in some Counties. Hedges and drystone walls are very British and we find both in Gloucestershire depending upon whether the land is high or low pasture. They are unique, they tell of our history and the origins of some are lost in the mists of time.

The word hedge comes from the Old English *hecg* and many other words in our language connect with the word hedge. We have hedgerow, hedgehog and hedge sparrow to name but a few.

Many hedges are nothing but old Parish boundaries or they show us where old droving roads were once used and even ancient watercourses. Sometimes they were remnants left from when a forest was cleared which means they represent great age indeed.

Many though were planted deliberately between 1750 and 1860 to comply with the Enclosures Act. The trees and shrubs were basically hawthorn, the lethal blackthorn with its wicked spikes, and the hazel with tree specimens like oak and elm.

Mixed hedgerows are of a much greater age. The orthodox method of dating a hedge is to count how many specimens of trees and shrubs are in it. The idea is that the number of species in a ten-yard length gives a rough and ready indication of general age.

In the past few years, we have lost 190,000 miles of these precious hedges with a devastating effect upon the flora and fauna. Some of our native species began to grow just after the last Ice Age, which was nine to ten thousand years ago and before the cross-Channel bridge vanished under the sea. Five thousand years ago migrating tribes brought seeds and saplings to add to what was already here.

Other specimens came in with the Romans for fruit and cattle fodder. From the Romans until 1600 there was a steady trickle of introductions some of which are now so well established we consider them indigenous.

True native trees are the juniper, birch, aspen, alder, hazel, cherry, willow, oak, elm and rowan and even more could be added to this list. Before 1600 the white and grey poplar were introduced as well as the wild pear, almond, peach, plum and two other types of elm. The list is exceedingly long and fascinating.

Since 1600 the newcomers have been the lime, the horse chestnut with its conkers loved by all boys, big as well as little, the scarlet oak, Chinese privet and monkey tree. Then in the nineteenth century there was another invasion from abroad with redwood and conifers from the West of America which also included the magnificent giant sequoia.

Most of these trees settled down quite happily with our soil and climate, though one or two sulked and had to be planted more carefully. So in many ways, these trees which grew in the middle of hedges, also tell us a little about our country's history.

A hedge of two yards in height is of enormous value to the wildlife. One of only half that height becomes dangerous to them. The birds can be targeted by predators, which makes nesting a hazardous occupation.

A tall hedge is difficult to trim and once allowed to grow unchecked soon becomes less valuable. It will grow gappy, draughty and make too much shade for crops. It could also lead to wind turbulence in the fields. The idea of trimming a hedge is not just to make it all neat and tidy, it is to make the hedge thick at the bottom and here it is well populated with insects and other small creatures. It is also vital to keep stock enclosed.

Field sheep must have a hedge at least one yard high. For cattle this should be up to 1.5 yards or rather more if the hedge has an "A" shape. Many farmers favour the "A" shape while others seem to prefer and insist upon the inverted "U"; some even go in for short back and sides with a flat top.

With the "A" shape, the trimmings are less likely to fall into the hedge and it is easier to leave promising saplings intact to grow on. Such a hedge receives the maximum sunlight and can easily shed a heavy fall of snow, which would destroy a flat-topped hedge.

A flail cutter is a downright menace even if it does save labour and wages. It butchers the trees and shrubs. It rips and renders the trunks and bark, so letting disease enter. Many such massacred stems will die back especially where the bark has been ripped ruthlessly.

An argument for flails, apart from saving money and labour, is that they chew up the growth to the benefit of the hedge and there is no laborious raking and burning afterwards.

A cut and layered hedge is a work of pure art. It is also incredibly beautiful and the wild life adores such. They can also be substantial against the cattle's pushes and shoves. Careful planning is needed though because hedging by the hedger is a most skilled country craft and not many people can do this now, sad to say.

The essence is to select appropriate trees in the hedge. Then make a quarter cut through the trunk, bend it sideways and leave a heel on the far side. This must be removed carefully to avoid water and disease setting up home.

A well cut and laid hedge only needs maintenance on an irregular basis with perhaps a proper relaying every so often. They end up objects of very great beauty and considerable strength.

A mixed hedge is the best but care must be taken not to include trees and shrubs which are lethally poisonous. Some dodgy ones are box, broom, cherry, laurel, laburnum, rhododendron and yew. The best trees for a hedge are beech, blackthorn, dogwood, hazel, hornbeam and field maple.

Where the soil is poor or trees thin on the ground, because

of altitude, like so many places in the Cotswolds, the answer is to go in for drystone walling. The Old English for such was dryge and many words in our language are connected. We have the stone waller in cricket, stone walling, stonechat for the bird and then there is stonemason. The Old English for stone is stan.

When exactly mortar was invented is very hard to say although it is almost certain the Palaeolithic and Neolithic people had figured out how to make this: perhaps around about 4,000 years BC.

Drystone walling is a remarkable craft which has not been spoiled by modernity and it too is another art form. Some of the walls around today are well over two centuries old and many may have even more distant roots. They have great merit and are very durable. They are quite stock proof and they take up very little land. They give good shelter in all weathers and can stand where it is impossible to drive in a fencing post.

They are cheap to maintain, drain themselves very well and can be climbed by a careful person. They need few tools to make, simply a four-pound hammer, a rough frame, a long piece of string for a straight line and – stones. They cannot, of course, be burned down either. Another plus point.

Drawbacks include the fact that they take time and considerable skill to erect. Clumsy people climbing over them will dislodge the top stones so the answer is to make a proper stile. If they should be near a rare tree, this might swing in a strong wind and the roots dislodge the wall's base. Nosy horses sometimes take it into their heads to smash the top stones off.

The stones are usually everywhere. A farmer with a lot in his field will be delighted to have them removed for wall building. It saves him from constantly shattering his plough shares.

Every stone should have three bearings. The wall should be wider at the base than at the top and it should stand in a foundation trench. Throughout the wall should be placed long, flat stones called the through stones. These add to stability and strength. The best stones, called the face stones, should be used on one side for beauty. The top stones are the copers and should be wedged in firmly against animals' rubbings.

Sometimes the top coping stones might be cemented in but this is very unwise. As the whole wall settles a gap might form in which at the top cracks would appear and then there could be a disaster. Top stones wedged in simply give the wall extra strength which makes the whole much superior.

A language has developed around drystone walling. In the Cotswolds the topping stone might be called the cap, cope or comb. If the wall is made from large and small stones which give a castellated effect, this may be known as Buck and Doe or Cock and Hen.

A small rectangular opening at the base of the wall can be left for exploring rabbits and the hunting fox. These too have some weird names depending upon which part of the country one visits. They range from rabbit smoots, penholes, pop holes, sheep smooses where the hole is large enough for sheep to transit and lunky hole, thawl hole plus cripple hole.

A locked top is where the cope consists of flattish stones set vertically on the top, while a batter is a wall which slopes backwards. Pins are small stones tapped into interspices as well as giving the whole more strength.

Sometimes great boulders are incorporated and these give tremendous strength yet it is perfectly feasible to build around them. Many a farmer has been quite overjoyed at getting rid of ghastly boulders in a field where he hopes to plough and grow a crop.

For many years drystone walling was sliding into the obscurity of a dying rural craft but now the Countryside Commission plus others are doing their best to invigorate a drystone walling campaign. They and others are doing this to make sure the beautiful craft of hedge-laying does not vanish altogether.

Hedges and drystone walls are our heritage. The wild life, the plants and flowers, all thrive on or near to them so we must cherish both hedge and wall and never allow them to disappear completely in this twenty-first century.

Abson

There can be few people who have not heard of Anna Sewell's book *Black Beauty*, even in our twenty-first century nuclear age. Many, though, may consider the work to be sentimental Victorian slush. But if that is the case, why does it live on? *Black Beauty* was written in a vastly different age to this and was a product of its time.

The daughter of Mary and Isaac Sewell, Anna, was born on 30th March 1820, in Great Yarmouth. When Anna was fourteen both her ankles were severely strained – injuries from which she never recovered. She was left an invalid for the rest of her life.

In those days, well-bred women were considered weak, prey to the vapours and incapable of handling their own affairs. They were chattels of fathers and husbands.

Anna's mother Mary, though, had backbone enough to stand out from the rest of her sex. She became famous in her own right with children's books because she did not take at all kindly to the Victorian male's chauvinistic behaviour.

Mary Sewell achieved considerable fame, which must have rubbed off on Anna. For some years they lived at Abson in south Gloucestershire at a property known as Blue Lodge. While there, Mary Sewell started a series of mothers' meetings which were held at nearby Wick. They were very popular and Anna would attend.

While at Blue Lodge, Anna saw a man killed by a cart, an incident she never forgot and which she incorporated into *Black Beauty*. From Abson, mother and daughter moved to Englishcombe Lane at Bath. It is not clear how long they lived there but ultimately they moved back to Norwich.

Because of her disability Anna could only get about on horseback, or by pony and trap. This was the age of the horse, as the railways had not yet moved into the powerful position they would eventually hold. Anna must have seen the most appalling sights, including cruelty to horses from savage treatment or starvation. These were carefully stored in her mind for her book.

She must also have pondered how a horse, through various changes of ownership, could go from being in great shape to almost being at death's door. This is vividly brought home in the book when Black Beauty meets Ginger for the last time.

Two practices in particular cut into Anna's heart. One was the savage and unnecessary practice of docking horses' tails. The excuse given was that the tail would not then get caught up in the harness, but carriage horses today don't have this problem. Perhaps the real root of the habit was pure fashion. A horse with no tail has no protection against biting flies.

The second evil was the use of the bearing rein. The well-off liked their carriage horses to hold their heads high, and they achieved this with the vicious bearing rein which, when attached to the bridle in a certain position, meant the horse could not stretch. Its head was clamped high, agonising the neck muscles. It was a cruel invention, and Anna fought it tooth and nail – with her pen.

Many call *Black Beauty* a semi-autobiographical work. Certainly Anna laboured long and hard at her only book. It took six years to write, mostly on scraps of paper when she was back in Norwich. It was her mother Mary who patiently wrote out the manuscript.

Black Beauty was published in 1877 and became an instant success. It was backed from the start by the Society for the Prevention of Cruelty to Animals, as it was known then. The Victorians swarmed to buy the book and it soon sold 100,000 copies. It was translated into French, Italian and German, a considerable feat for those days. But Anna did not live long after her book came out, dying in 1878. *Black Beauty* was her only work but it is doubtful if even she realised what an effect it was to have on people. It has been filmed and the story remains evergreen. Above all, it is a social history of the way people lived. What an epitaph for Anna Sewell.

Almondsbury

Almondsbury is a dainty little village set below a hilltop facing the west and the River Severn.

It has always been a fairly large parish which consisted of four tithings. Almondsbury itself was in the Lower Berkeley Hundred while three other parishes lie elsewhere.

Some of its early names were Almodesberie, Almudebit and Alkemundesbury. From the Old English we have the name Aepelmod which was often shortened to Almod.

Burgh usually means a fortified place so we may guess the whole translates to Aepelmod's fortified home.

Certainly there was a Roman camp on the top of the hill, which is understandable.

Even today the views are magnificent. They take in the river, the bridges, the Forest of Dean and the Welsh hills.

For defensive and scouting purposes such a camp would be invaluable. At the same time it was very accessible to Glevum, today's Gloucester. Easy marching distance for the tough, battle hardened legions.

Such a fort in this position would control the whole area, little places like Carrybrook, Gaunt's Earthcott, Easter Compton, Over and Patchway. These little places also had their early names. Cadibroc or Cattybrook meant simply a brook which belonged to Cada.

Gaunt's Earthcott's earlier names were Herdicate and Erdecot, which meant bluntly just an earth cottage – probably some primitive hovel which belonged to a poor peasant or slave family.

Easter Compton was Estore Astit which tells us there was a farmstead in a valley, while Over was known earlier as Ofre or Ouram – both words mean a slope.

Patchway had a multitude of names. A few are Petsage, Petteslaw and Patchow. This is thought to translate to mean Peot's enclosure.

Hempton's name has hardly changed from Hemton while Hampton meant a high farmstead. Hortham was simply Horthame which means the place where whortleberries grew. It is from the fairly rare Old English horte.

As to Almondsbury itself we have a bit of a mystery. Rudder's magnificent work on Gloucestershire hints that the name could descend from Alcmund. He was a West Saxon prince, the father of Ecbert or Egbert who some historians claim was the first king of the English. Others question this though.

The tribes then were still deliriously happy to fight each other at the drop of a hat so how could they hope to agree upon an overall king? It is most likely he was king of the most powerful tribe at that time. This often see-sawed between the Mercians and Wessex.

There is another mysterious tradition which says that Offa, king of the Mercians, was actually buried in this region and was found by the people in 1650. Now we have another historical dispute, because some sages insist Offa was interred at Bedford. Where is the proof though?

Because the ordinary people were said to have discovered the tomb, Rudder becomes positively scathing, which is rather surprising. It is true the ordinary people would lack education or literacy but they had brains and tongues.

Who is to say they were wrong? Look at the stories which have descended to us from word of mouth alone. Further, they had nothing at all to gain from romantic lies.

It is fairly certain the bones, which were found at a tumulus, a burial mound or barrow, were of two distinct men. One was reputed to be very large. The bones were enclosed in a huge stone coffin, so skilfully made that the joints were not, at first, discernible. The stone which covered the coffin was described as ponderously heavy, of a grey colour with some red intermixed. It was also studded with some shining substance.

Two coins were also discovered which simply add to the mystery. One had the impression of a falcon while there was a head on the second. Some historians think the head was that of Claudius Caesar.

If this is so, this gives us a Roman date but, in that case, why were the bones not burned? Why did the tomb lack an inscription?

If they were Offa's bones how and why did a Roman coin get in? At this period, Christianity had touched English shores and it was pretty unlikely a man like Offa would have welcomed a Roman coin in his tomb.

One old record says the bones were those of a huge man but how big is huge? In those days, men were smaller than us now. Their diet was nowhere near as good as ours. They would be more riddled with disease especially the likes of arthritis and rheumatism, all of which shrink bones on to each other and lower height.

One skeleton was supposed to be more than three feet taller than normal – or had the bones been displaced?

Another puzzling feature is that the bodies were buried in a sitting position. This is most significant because it was a position only adopted for the high and mighty. It was regarded as an emblem of eternity only used for the exalted, which would include a king like Offa.

Where are these bones now? A blank wall was unfortunately met in this investigation which is not all that surprising at this great time distance. Time marches on though.

When the Severn flooded all those centuries ago it did it with a vengeance. No concrete barriers to control its waters. So much of the land was marshy. A figure is given of 1,342 acres always liable to flood when the Severn had one of its fits for causing general mayhem.

Tockington, for example, in this tithing, is only mentioned as having marshy lands which speaks for itself. The whole estate belonged to the Berkeleys.

An abbey was founded in 1148 in Bristol and Robert Fitzharding endowed it with Almondsbury as well as other estates. It is certain this Abbey held the village with a court leet. These were rather important local courts, probably a kind of forerunner of our magistrates' courts. All the residents attended before the lord or his steward and the petty offences were dealt with as well as general administration for the district.

There was a fair and a market. The former was held on Whit Monday and ran for six days while the weekly market was held on Wednesdays. The judges of those days had a good say in what went on, where and when. If they considered markets and fairs unnecessary they were halted and there were no arguments either.

Henry VIII saw the Abbey dissolved with so many others and the village changed hands a number of times. It went back into the Berkeley family for a short while through marriage, then out again when it belonged to a Bristol merchant.

Gradually it was broken up and sold piecemeal. From the start of the twentieth century it reverted once more to a quiet little village, minding its own business. Towards the end of that century though, concrete descended upon it.

The first motorway flyover was built nearby.

Now motorists scoot past on their way here and there. How many know the little village near the bottom of the hill still holds an unsolved mystery. How many of those who live there know this either?

Badminton

Badminton and Grumbalds Ash have always nestled together like egg and bacon, each with ancient names. Of the two,

Grumbalds Ash has the magnificent record of thirty-two with a multiplicity of spellings which range over a few hundred years.

Four of these are Grimbaldess, Brimoldeshashdr, Grymboldesse and Grimbodeshach. A round translation says they all mean Grumbald's meeting place or ash.

Who was Grumbald? We have no idea. Certainly his name became that of the Hundred for quite a large region although originally it had been called the Hundred of Aggemed or Agmead. Perhaps we may presume Grumbald may have been someone of consequence for his name to predominate.

At this early part of our history, the area would not be as we know it today. It would have been more heavily treed, and a Hundred was calculated to be enough land to keep 100 families and their animals. This explains why it covered such a large area. It also meant the lord had the right to call 100 warriors when he needed them.

Where was Grumbalds Ash? This is the jackpot question. Some people hold it was destroyed when Badminton Park was made.

This is erroneous because the archaeological records state quite firmly the village's site had not yet been discovered. Many villages did disappear like that of the famous Brunanburh, and the culprit was usually the plague. Everyone simply died from the disease and nature took over again.

We know that when the Romans appeared, the tribe of the region was that of the Dubonii. To the Romans they were nothing but savage barbarians.

In reality they were quite cultured and were one of three tribes who minted their own currency from a centre near to Cirencester. Where the Romans were concerned it was simply another culture clash but though the Britons were good fighters, they lacked the power and discipline of Rome.

Some historians think at this time, many of the tribes dispensed with kings and became republicans instead. The jury is still out on this one though.

The records are pretty certain that the Romans energetically built one of their marvellous roads, part of which ran directly past Badminton to Dunkirk and the Sodbury camp, which is logical. Rome insisted upon communications at all times.

Badminton already existed with only five old names, three of which are Badimyncgtun, Madmintyne and Badynton. It is considered this means a farmstead associated with Baduhelm or Badu from the Old English. Rudder, who wrote the great book of the Shire in the eighteenth century, refuses to be drawn but, perhaps tongue-in-cheek, says the word comes from bevan to pray and moizn a monk. He even goes on to suggest this signifies a priest's town but the argument against this is Madminton in Domesday.

There is an unusual, ancient legend which holds that no "snake, adder or lizard" has ever been found in the Hundred. This sounds very far-fetched, even for those distant days, yet for decades residents held these creatures were exceedingly rare.

Fossils have been found of both the oyster and periwinkle as well as a round stone, loosely called a bullet stone, so we are sure this land was once deep under some ancient sea.

After a few centuries the land was home to the Hwicce tribe who were forced to pay tribute to the more powerful Mercians.

That all of these people did exist is proven by air photographs in which it is easy to pick out the ancient field systems.

There are even Celtic fields detectable from old RAF pictures which show earthworks which also hint at quarrying, as well as old ridge and furrow ploughing methods. Banks can be seen which were used for division purposes with the old "strip" method of land allocation.

Interestingly, these old records are also adamant that somewhere near to today's Badminton there is a long vanished Roman villa. It is reasonable to assume this would have belonged to the commander of the Cohors Auxiliaria Equitata as "agents in rebus" of the code of Theodosius. The officers may have served with the II Legion and become eligible for mastering other services owing to their smart training and general reputation.

Rudder is firm in that Oswald founded the monastery of Pershore in Worcestershire and gave several tenements of Badminton to this monastery.

In the reign of Edward the Confessor, Edrick was the lord and held Badminton then Ernulf de Hesding owned it in the reign of William I. It was taxed at four hides – and 100 hides made up the Hundred.

There were eight acres of meadow plus fifteen plough tillages and the yearly rent was ten shillings. It also held nine slaves.

Ernulf de Hesding died and left an heir who was a minor. His guardians held a portion of Badminton for when he attained his majority. In 1170 half of this was ordered by the king to be paid to the daughter of William fitz Alan upon her marriage. Why? Again we do not know.

Some of the records suggest this Hesding did not enjoy his life for long because he was hanged by King Stephen. His alleged offence was that in 1138 he protracted the defence of his nephew, another William fitz Allan – but with an extra 'L' now – at the castle of Shrewsbury. How true is this though?

There is another story that a person of this very name witnessed Queen Maud's Charters. These created Milo, Earl of Hereford and Geoffrey de Magnaville, Earl of Essex in 1141. If so, this Hesding was a man of some importance but the records are very sparse. There could possibly have been two men with the same name which was not unknown in those days.

⥼⥽

The next family upon the Badminton scene was that of Boteler. Ralph Boteler lived in the reign of Henry II. He held the office of butler to Robert Boteler, Earl of Mellent and Leicester.

He settled at Overfly in Warwickshire, founded a monastery there of Benedictine monks in the fifth year of Stephen's Reign.

They were a family of note because another Boteler became the Justice of the Assize in 1225. It was the next of the line who lived at Badminton. He married a daughter whose ancestors had been Barons of Wem since the conquest.

The records tell us that Ralph died 'seized' of Badminton. One Boteler called Adam was the High Sheriff of Gloucestershire in 1270, Another, Sir Thomas, married into the family of Alan Earl of Arundel and this brought the name of Allan into the family.

The Botelers held Badminton for about 400 years, then we come to the Somersets.

The manors of Great and Little Badminton were purchased in 1612 by Edward, the fourth Earl of Worcester, in order to settle them on his son Sir Thomas Somerset, Viscount Cashel, upon his marriage in 1617.

His heiress, daughter Elizabeth, died unwed. She gave the whole to Henry Somerset, Lord Herbert, afterwards the Duke of Beaufort. This Duke's pedigree goes back to John of Gaunt, the third surviving son of Edward III.

John of Gaunt had four children with Katherine, widow of Sir John Swynford. Later she became his wife and he gave the name Beaufort to this family, legitimised after his marriage. The name Beaufort came from a castle in Anjou.

All the family have held high office and been created earls and dukes. They had close connections with the royal families of England and Scotland and one became the mother of Henry VII. Henry, the third Duke of Somerset, gained great honours in the wars with France. He took the castle at Anjou, put 300 Scots to the sword and then hanged all the French who remained inside.

In the Wars of the Roses he adhered to the House of Lancaster, was taken prisoner at the battle of Hexham and beheaded in 1464. All he left behind was a son, Charles, who took the name of Somerset from his father's title. Again there was no heir and so ended the legitimate line of John of Gaunt.

Charles Somerset had great ability and lived on to high honours. He became a privy councillor to Henry VII, and Admiral of the Fleet, was created a Knight Bannerett in 1497, was nominated Knight of the Garter and was employed by Henry VII and Henry VIII on important embassies.

He married Elizabeth, Baroness Herbert in her own right, the only daughter and heir of William Herbert, Earl of Huntingdon, Lord Herbert of Raglan, Chepstow and Gower. In consequence of his marriage he bore the title of Lord Herbert. Because of his services to the royal family in 1514 he was created Earl of Worcester by patent from Henry VIII. He died in 1526.

Not all the family did so well. Henry was the second Earl of Worcester, famed for his noted exploits in the wars with France. He married another Elizabeth and had four sons. His son Thomas died in the tower in 1587. Another died in France in 1529 and Francis was slain by the Scots at Musselborough Field.

William, the third Earl, was one of the peers who sat at the trial of Mary, Queen of the Scots while Edward, the fourth Earl became master of the horse under Elizabeth I and was considered the best horseman and tilter in the country.

The fifth Earl Henry had a great fortune but spent a lot of this on the royal cause in the Civil wars for which he was created Marquis of Worcester. He kept the castle of Raglan and held it against the Parliamentary forces with a garrison of 800 men from 1642 to 1646. He eventually had to cede to Sir Thomas Fairfax who besieged it. This was all done with great honour until baseness set in. He was taken into custody by Black Rod and died in December. His castle was demolished and all the timber in his three parks valued at £100,000. This family lost a fortune in the royal cause and not all was restored at the Restoration either.

Much more was gone than land. The fifth Earl's grandson was Henry Somerset who married the wealthy widow Mary Capel, Lady Beauchamp who was six feet tall. It was not a love match, yet their marriage lasted for forty years and they showed each other much affection.

Henry had brains. He did not hesitate to ingratiate himself

with Parliament and was also swift to support the Restoration of Charles II and who can blame him for such pragmatism. He succeeded in recovering much of the family land but received no financial compensation. He was a staunch supporter of the Stuarts and was made a Knight of the Garter, a privy councillor and, in 1682, Duke of Beaufort.

He supported James II against William of Orange and after 1688 his influence was much reduced and he retired to Badminton. His clever wife had always kept meticulous accounts and it was she who managed the estate in his absence. In 1678 when rumours flew around that the French were about to invade, this gallant lady promptly raised militia in Bristol.

Badminton was inherited by Lord Herbert from his cousin in 1655 and it was made the family seat. Rebuilding of the house started in 1663.

Mary improved the property with formal gardens and landscaped walks. She was a recognised botanist and collector of exotic plants. She had the idea of installing what she called stoves and these gave the heat which eventually led to Mary having more than a thousand rare specimens.

Working as a great team the pair finally restored the family wealth and established an estate for their heirs for the next 300 years. Not many marriages can have brought such fruition.

The estate is approximately 20,000 acres. There is an eighteenth-century church rebuilt from around 1783 to 1785. There is a plantation of trees known as the birthday trees of cedar, silver fir and cypress. Each has been planted on the birthday of a Beaufort. There are twenty-four in all, each of which has a zinc nameplate. There are also two other famous oak trees in the park. One is called the FitzHerbert Oak and is thirty-seven feet around. The second is the Duchess Oak and is slightly smaller.

Charlotte, the wife of the fifth Duke had thirteen children and her life is remembered by a white marble tablet in the church. There is also a tablet to Lord Raglan who died during the siege of Sebastopol. This man has been as much maligned as Haig after the First World War, but a close study shows that the butchery of the infamous charge of the Light Brigade was not really his fault. It was apparently another who did not deliver a clear message which sent the gallant 600 to their inevitable slaughter.

Deer hunting has always been a popular sport of the Dukes of Beaufort but it is said that in 1762 after a poor day's sport, hounds were put into Silk Wood. They flushed out a fox and so started fox hunting. Will Long was a legendary huntsman who served under four dukes and is always remembered in connection with hunting at Badminton.

One day when the weather was inclement, the duke decided to play tennis in the picture gallery. It became enthusiastic to the detriment of the pictures so the Duke brought out a shuttle. This was used instead of a ball and was derived from a game played by officers in India known as Poona. The Duke's game was known as shuttlecock and battledore, but now it is simply called badminton.

Badminton village in the meantime continued as it had for centuries. There was no cottage industry connected with it, unlike others in the region. The village was tied to the land and farming. The tenants though, were quite an unusual bunch.

The price of corn had soared so high that on 3rd October 1795, twenty-five male tenants and one woman put their signatures to an important document which they published in a broadsheet. These tenants stated quite unequivocally that wheat was not to be sold at a higher price than nine shillings a bushel which was then roughly 9.5 gallons. Neither would they sell their wheat to jobbers or corn dealers.

Instead it would only be allowed to go to millers and bakers for sale to the public at a reasonable profit. Small quantities were to be sold to any person in the neighbourhood. If the marked price became lower they would lower their prices accordingly. They would thrash at the usual time of year, about 1st November. To prevent a scarcity, they also recommended a mixture of barley be put with the wheat which could be passed onto poor labourers and the destitute. This was a remarkable example of helping the have-nots in society.

Badminton village was obviously much loved. In those days people were apt to be born, live and die in the same place.

Some, though, did break from this mould and travel. There is a wistful, rather poignant poem which was published privately in the nineteenth century by someone who left the region.

The little book called simply *Poems* by E M Bethell went into limited circulation in 1854. The poem has eight verses and the source is *Glos Notes and Queries Volume IV,* page 70.

Just before this period, a certain Mr Vizard, who worked as a chimney sweep, often went hunting with the Beaufort hounds. He became quite a famous person and knew he could always borrow a decent mount from the seventh Duke. He became known as the Hunting Chimney Sweep. Nimrod, the great sporting writer of the times, noted that at a meet of 300 foxhunters, none was quite as famous or as generally popular as Mr Vizard. How about that for democracy?

In 1836 a table shows that 271 people were employed by the 'big house'.

These people ranged from those who worked in the house itself to the stables, kennels, the garden, the game parks plus the farming bailiffs and tradesmen.

There were thirty-nine people connected with the horses in the magnificent courtyard stables' area.

At one time Badminton had its own fire brigade with a horse-drawn engine. Two horses were kept specifically for this purpose. Most fires were of the hay and straw variety. This brigade was disbanded in the twentieth century between the wars.

Badminton Station opened in 1903. The eighth Duke obtained a concession. In return for allowing the Great Western Railway to cut through his estate, he obtained the right for 'non-stop' trains to halt at Badminton to set down parties of visitors. This was closed in 1968 under the Doctor Beeching plan.

During the Second World War Queen Mary lived at Badminton, which caused some problems. She was an old lady then but rather imperious and she could not stand being bored. She ended up being held in great affection by all the villagers as well as the many service personnel stationed round and about. She was very quick to help others. She spent a considerable time sorting papers in the Muniment Room and she arranged the cataloguing of its contents. She is reputed to have organised a 'Wooding Squad' and she waged war against ivy and other plant parasites. She attended the lectures supposedly laid on just for the troops. This very remarkable old lady was into everything and adored for it.

After the 1948 Olympics the 10th Duke became deeply interested in the new 'sport' of eventing. So was born the Three Day Event at Badminton now known world-wide by the village name alone.

The first event caused the Duke much worry. Would anyone turn up to watch and compete? It was all rather a gamble for him in throwing open his park. There were 478 entries for the first Badminton with 22 starters.

The first prize was £150 and the entry fee was £2 per horse. The 'office' was sited in Colonel Horn's house and his piano doubled up as a filing cabinet. The grandstand seats were bales of straw and wagons. Many people watched by standing on their cars. It was all incredibly laid back. The first winner was Golden Willow owned by Mrs Home Kidson and ridden by John Shedden.

Today's Badminton Horse Trials are world-famous and many countries compete. It is also considered the ideal test for horse and rider prior to the Olympics. Now it is very professional and there is a magic ring to the name of Badminton.

What is the village like today? It is a gem of a place, beautifully kept and a treat to visit. Near to the entrance of the 'big house' there are some buildings which are worth careful study.

The almshouses were founded by the first Duchess and date from 1705.

High up, in the centre, there is the Beaufort coat of arms. On either side are two lozenges which are the arms of the first Duchess as widow in which the Beaufort arms are impaled with the Capel arms.

They were the Earls of Essex and her family.

There is a tranquillity about Badminton Village, yet there is also activity from the people who reside there.

Horses proliferate still and when the Badminton Horse Trials are held, the village throbs with vigorous life as riders and horses, from points all over the world, attend to compete.

The logistics involved in catering for multiple two and four legs are quite mind-boggling, yet Badminton does not turn a hair. It thrives instead.

Long may villages like this last in England. They are part of our ancient heritage.

Barnsley

Barnsley and Bibury have nearly always been lumped together like sibling villages which is quite understandable as they are so near to each other. Like all of our villages, Barnsley has had its share of old names which total twenty-one in all. Two of them are Bearmodes Lea and Berandestag. This means Beormod's glade or clearing and comes from the Old English personal nouns of Beornmod and Leah. We have no idea at all who these people were.

As usual, the Romans were there stamping around in their new ownership and it seems they must have preferred Barnsley because they built a good villa there. Whether this displaced some ancient Briton or they lived cheek by jowl with one is unknown. Not very likely though because the Romans despised the Britons because they did not bathe. It is more likely they would have kept themselves highly aloof from the 'natives'. If there was any kind of thin alliance it would certainly have been an uneasy one.

We do know this villa had a very large agricultural system which indicates it was rather self-sufficient; always prudent when living in occupied territory even if there were soldiers around for defence. When this villa was excavated a Roman floor was discovered which held interesting evidence. There were Roman cart wheel tracks across what had obviously been some kind of farmyard which had, in turn, been floored with stone by the Roman occupier. When measured these tracks were found to be exactly 4 feet and 8.5 inches which we call the 'standard' gauge. This titbit of information raises a pertinent question because Isambard Kingdom Brunel used this particular measurement for his railway's standard gauge. Did he get his width from here or is the whole thing just a very remarkable coincidence?

Domesday gives us quite a bit more information. Barnsley was in the Hundred of Rapsgate though Bibury had its own Hundred but this may have been for nothing more sinister than administrative reasons.

Durand the sheriff of Gloucestershire held both and lots more land besides, all from the bishop and church of Worcester. This made Durand a man of considerable consequence. At Barnsley he held three hides and one virgate of land which included twelve villages, six ploughs and twelve slaves. This is rather a top heavy number of slaves for residents but it is also tied in with another land owner.

The church at Bibury held twenty-one hides with nineteen villagers, two smallholders, three riding men who each had four hides and ploughs. There was a priest, eleven male and female slaves plus two mills all of which states that at the time of Domesday, Bibury was the larger village and more go-ahead.

These entries are surprisingly not quite as forthcoming as usual with the Book and straightaway raise a huge question. When William I sent off three clerks to conduct his great survey it was with the sole object of finding out exactly what his conquest had given to him.

The snag was these clerks could hardly, if ever, speak the Britons' tongue. The British were in a similar situation so it is quite possible tiny details were missed simply because of lack of language. Much may have, quite innocently, been written down in error.

William I had a devious mind, rather untrusting too. Once the clerks had gone on their way he carefully sent a second lot after them. This bunch were to check upon the first clerks to make quite sure there was no hanky panky. The language problem would still remain though and although the second bunch of clerks made sure there was no favouritism by the first for backhanders, they would fare little better language-wise. It is distinctly possible clerks from both groups ended getting a little tangled up. Especially when trying to question awkward Britons who resented them being there in the first place.

William did read some of his book but as it was such a huge tome there would be little chance at all he could wade through it all. Especially as, by then, he only had one year left to live when he started the whole exercise.

In Domesday Rapsgate is referred to also as the Hundred of Begesberie in places, so interested readers must simply take their pick.

Not long after the Conquest, the whole large estate and manor came into the hands of the Fitz-Herberts. Certainly Peter Fitz-Herbert was 'seized' of it in the reign of Henry III. This man married the third daughter and coheir of William de Braos, Baron of Brecknock. He, in turn, was succeeded by his son Herbertus then a brother took the estate. It went down to John who was the last of the line to own Barnsley.

We do know that Hugh le Dispenser had a charter of free warren which was in due course settled upon his son.

Unfortunately for the family, the son was attainted of high treason so the estate was forfeited back to the crown.

Edward III gave it to Edmund, Earl of Kent who was the grandson of Edward I. There were the usual deaths until it came down to Joan, commonly known as The Fair Maid of Kent. She married the Black Prince so became mother to Edward II.

She must have been quite a remarkable lady because she was twice married, twice divorced yet kept her estate and her head upon her slender neck. Unusual for those very savage times.

Once again the Barnsley manor and estate descended downwards to appropriate heirs which, in one instance, was Thomas Holland, Earl of Kent, Joan's son by her first marriage. There was another son Thomas who was beheaded at Cirencester in the reign of Henry IV. It was always dangerous and even lethal to back the incorrect royal horse in throne disputes or religious matters.

The manor stayed in the Holland family before moving to that of the Mortimers, again through marriage. An estate like that of Barnsley would be very attractive for any man of blood who fancied bettering himself.

Richard, Duke of York, heir to the crown, also became Barnsley's heir but he was killed at the battle of Wakefield in the last year of Henry VI.

Barnsley went on down through the families until it was bought outright by William Bouchier in 1608. Finally getting to more 'modern' times it became vested in Mrs Cassandra Perrot. This all shows what a chequered history Barnsley has had. It must all have been very disconcerting to the peasants whose lives were dominated just by whosoever owned the estate. They had precious few rights indeed, if any at all, and were always at the beck, call and mercy of the lord in ownership.

Barnsley mansion and park were not built until the eighteenth century though it is recognised there had been a residence of some kind or other, for past families. The name of the architect is highly uncertain so best classed as unknown though there is a remote chance it might have been Thornhill. Some old people declare two men were involved but proof is difficult to find.

It is a Baroque building from about 1700 when the owner is recorded as being Brerton Bouchier. When he died his daughter inherited and, though still a minor, married Henry Perrot of Oxfordshire. Many hold it was Bouchier who started the park and it was Perrot who completed it with revised plans. The cellars do show where walls have been tampered with which also relates to a previous building.

The stone in the construction came from Barnsley's own quarry, now long since disused. It is golden-grey in colour and beautiful in the sun. The plasterer was William Taylor and James Millard of Gloucester was the Clerk of the Works though the latter was also well-known for his church monuments.

The magnificent library walls were designed and decorated by Nash in 1806 to 1810 in the Empire style and history was made again. One day, inside this library, were found Isaac Newton's books which had lain unrecognised for a considerable period. How did they get there in the first place? This can only lie in the realms of conjecture.

Nash appears to have had his hands into everything because Bibury Lodge, called familiarly the Pepper Pot, was also designed by him.

Barnsley Park was the home of a lady who was internationally recognised as one of the great gardeners, writers and broadcasters.

Barnsley has come a very long way since the Roman days with a multiplicity of owners yet it is exceedingly famous now for its fabulous gardens and the house as well as history in general, all of which slot neatly into each other. Perhaps one would be lost without the other; certainly our general history would be the poorer.

Berkeley

Today Berkeley might look like simply another English small town which just happens to have its own castle – but how deceptive looks are. There is so much more to Berkeley than can hope to meet the eye.

It had twenty-one names both before and after the Conquest, among which are Berclonga, On Beore, Lea and Bercgalai. They all, one way or another, mean a clearing of birch trees, while Berclinga refers to monks who once inhabited the place.

It had its legends also. There was a woman called the witch of Berkeley, who, it was reputed, gave her soul to Beelzebub. She repented, but it was all rather late in the day for her.

The story goes that she lived in the ninth century and her original tale is thought to come from William of Malmesbury. She was at dinner one day when a raven came and started to chatter to her. She went ashen and said, "This is the day the plough comes home."

She hastily sent for her son and daughter. He was a priest, she a nun. She implored them to pray for her and gave specific after-death orders. They were to sew her body into a stag's skin, place it in a stone coffin, which had bands of iron. It was then to be bound with three enormous chains.

After she died, her children did just this. On the first night, a demon broke one of the chains. On the second night, another chain was shattered. On the third night, a terrible demon broke the third chain and commanded the witch's body to rise. The corpse rose slowly. Outside a black horse waited. The demon sprang upon it, swept the witch up behind him and galloped off into the darkness. As she found herself being carried to Hell the witch uttered great shrieks which were heard four miles away. This story was told in verse, with some added Gothic touches for good measure, by Robert Southey.

One other legend is about the Berkeley toad, carved in stone in the medieval church. It depicts a toad clutching two human heads and was supposed to be kept in the castle dungeons and to have fed upon prisoners' bodies. Most likely this was simply a horror story to make children behave.

Centuries ago, Berkeley did well for markets. It had a monthly one for cheese and cattle and a weekly market for diary produce. Barges used to anchor at Berkeley Pill with cargoes of coal and stone at Stock.

On voting days, a man could have as much free beer as he could manage to drink. Sometimes recruiting sergeants would visit the town wearing flashy uniforms. They would have a spiel, with lots of big talk about a splendid man's life in the army and there would always be the bait of the monarch's shilling.

Domesday says the town was in the Berkeley Hundred and King Edward held five hides. There were five ploughs, twenty villagers, five smallholders, nine slaves and two mills, so it was never exactly insignificant.

John Smyth was a great historian and steward of the Berkeleys. He wrote an account of the Hundred of Berkeley – up until perhaps even recent times many locals were called Hundreders. He was a good servant and lived at Nibley. He wrote the Berkeley Manuscripts, as well as a catalogue of men and Armour in Glos in 1608. This typescript remained in the muniment room at the castle for twenty-five years until printed, at last, under the editorship of Sir John Maclean in 1885. Smyth was three years younger than Shakespeare, but outlived him by twenty-five years.

Unfortunately, Smyth's pedigree of the Berkeley family can be disputed. He held they began with Harding, son to the King of Denmark, who was rewarded with Berkeley for his services at Hastings.

It is held much more likely that Robert Fitzharding, the reeve of Bristol and a rich merchant, was granted the manor in 1153. He was the son of Harding, a Bristol magistrate. William of

Malmesbury said of him, "He was better used to whet his tongue in strife than to wield arms in war."

The House of Robert Fitzharding held Berkeley Castle for more than seven centuries. It is fairly certain that Robert descended in the male line from Eadnoth, the 'Staller' of Edward the Confessor and Harold, son of Godwine. The latter fell in battle against the son of another Harold.

He founded the monastery of St Augustine's in Bristol. When the empress Matilda and her son, later to be Henry II, lived at Bristol Castle, Robert was their great friend and supporter, ever quick to put his great wealth at their disposal.

Henry II had an elephant's memory and when he came to power, he did not forget. He granted Robert Fitzharding the Manor of Berkeley and gave permission for a castle to be built. So in 1086, he held land in the area in pledge of Brictric, a man not exactly loved by Matilda because he had rejected her hand in matrimony. Some historians think he may even have held this land before that time, which upsets Smyth's pedigree history of the family.

Berkeley's origins are rather confused and tangled. The former lord of Berkeley was Roger, who was simply thrown out. Partly this was because he refused to pay rent to this king, but also because he had supported Stephen when the crown was hotly disputed between Stephen and Matilda.

Roger considered himself the rightful owner of the manor and he was forced to retire to his other castle at Dursley in 'high dudgeon'. However, there is another story, which holds he became a kind of Robin Hood. Certainly, he did harass Fitzharding so much that the latter had to ask the king to intervene.

Matters were eventually settled in the time-honoured way of those days with marriages. Maurice Fitzharding took in marriage Roger's daughter. Roger's son had to marry Robert's daughter. Obviously, none of the four young people were consulted. Politics were of far more importance than young lovers' feelings.

It was Maurice's grandson, another Robert, who joined the

baronial party against King John. For his pains he was excommunicated and his castle seized by John. It appears there was some awful muddle, because this Robert is sometimes known as Robert de Brackle. Brackley was the headquarters of the barons at this time.

Robert died without issue and was succeeded by his brother Thomas. We then get many first names going down the tree of descent until we come to another Thomas who is considered the first baron proper. He eventually was taken prisoner at the Battle of Bannockburn and died in 1321.

It seems the family was not always wise when it came to taking sides. One sided with the confederacy of the barons against the Despensers and took part in ravaging the Welsh Marches. He and the Mortimers were forced to submit to the king and this family member was imprisoned until he died in 1326.

At the battle of Poitiers, one young knight became famous for his gallantry and courage, but it led to his capture. Some records insist this was another Maurice, while a second source argues it had to be Thomas, lord of Berkeley.

⊰⊱⋊⋉⊰⊱

For many years the Berkeley family was very close friends with a family called the Veels. This friendship lasted for 250 years. The men together made pilgrimages to the Holy Land. They fought the French side by side. They raided deer as companions in Painswick Park. In short, they were the original buddy-buddies.

But friendship ended when enmity came between Lord Berkeley and Viscount Lisle. Living halfway between these two arguing barons was Robert Veel. He was forced to take sides and chose the Lisles. He tried to capture Berkeley Castle by bribing the gatekeeper, but this grandiose idea failed when somebody talked. The outcome of it all was the last real pitched battle fought on English soil at Nibley Green.

One Berkeley was Sir William who, for a time, was governor of Virginia. Nothing lasts though and the title became vacant in the eighteenth century. Charles II created a second son of the line, Baron Berkeley, though the earldom as we think of it became vacant in 1665.

The title was revived in 1803 in favour of Henry Somerset, fifth Duke of Beaufort. It is all rather convoluted because the castle and its occupants always seemed to be involved in high drama and terror.

Perhaps the most ghastly happening involved Edward II. This young monarch picked himself dubious friends and none more so than Hugh Despenser. He gravely offended the Marchers who considered their own customs far more sacred than any royal ones. In 1321 there was violent revolution. It ended with Edward's queen living in open adultery with Mortimer, plotting against her husband.

She decided England must have a new king, their son – also Edward. In 1327 a full parliament held that Edward II was incompetent to rule. He was forced to abdicate in favour of his son.

Now we come to the horror bit. Edward was taken to Berkeley castle and imprisoned there. Everyone wanted him to die nice and quietly, so smoothing the new royal path. Edward, though, had other ideas. He simply was not prepared to turn up his toes.

Despite being kept in barbaric conditions, without food and water and in a deep, wet and fetid cell, he would not die. Se here was an impasse. He had to be made to die – and without a mark on his body, so his death would seem 'natural'.

Maurice, the then Lord Berkeley, was reputed to be a humane man. He went away for a few days and whether this was intentional or not, we will never know. Once he was out of sight and mind, Edward's two vicious jailers acted. They heated a poker until it glowed red-hot then, without mercy, compunction or even hesitation, they rammed it up Edward's bowel. It is said that his screams could be heard all over the village.

In due course Maurice was tried for regicide. However, he was found innocent so Edward III took the crown, as there was 'no mark on his father's body'. Whether he was part of the plot is unknown; perhaps not.

This castle has had its troubled history down the centuries, but today is considered the oldest castle in England with a continually living family.

The Berkeleys though are not the only famous family. In 1749 a baby was born whose life would affect the whole of mankind and for which all of us, even today, should give thanks.

Oddly enough, he was another Edward and his surname was Jenner. He was one of six children born to Stephen Jenner. His mother came from the Head family and her father had been the village vicar. Jenner's own father died when he was five and it was his older brother, Stephen, who dealt with his education.

At the age of eight he was packed off to school at Wotton-under-Edge, later to that of Dr Washbourn, of Cirencester. It seems Edward Jenner was the Sir David Attenborough of those times – he had an affinity with natural history.

Edward Jenner became apprenticed to Daniel Ludlow, of Sodbury, surgeon. In 1770 he went to London as a resident pupil in the home of the great John Hunter. It was here he received his great education and started up a sincere lifelong friendship with Hunter. They both thrived on all matters scientific and got on famously.

It was on Hunter's recommendation that Jenner was allowed to prepare the specimens brought back in 1771 from Cook's voyage. At the same time he pursued ardent studies at St George's Hospital and then in 1773 returned to practice in Berkeley, living with his elder brother. He soon became a medical success.

He was a man of myriad interests, which included not only his botanical and ornithological studies, but he also collected fossils, played the flute and violin and even found time to write poems.

Hunter particularly encouraged him in natural history, especially that concerning the cuckoo and fossils in general. One of his papers confirmed that the cuckoo became boss of the nest by the simple expedient of pushing the other chicks out. It is thought Jenner's nephew Henry was the observer.

In 1794 Jenner contracted typhus rather badly but recovered, and turned his fertile mind to cowpox. He knew that milkmaids who caught this never later contracted the dreadful smallpox. "Why not?" he asked.

Smallpox was a dreadful, feared scourge which, if it did not kill, left a person so maimed and disfigured they had to become recluses because of their hideous looks. None were exempt.

Jenner was a brave man with the courage of his convictions. On 14th May 1796, he vaccinated an eight-year-old boy with lymph taken from a girl who had cowpox.

The boy developed cowpox. On 1st July he took an enormous gamble and inoculated the boy for a second time, but from a genuine smallpox case. The boy did not contract the feared disease. Jenner considered he had proved his argument and wrote a paper. This did not get into print, so in 1798 he published a much fuller edition of his observations of experiments. This is now considered a classic among all medical books world-wide. Jenner stated unequivocally that cowpox definitely protected against smallpox and he gave details of twenty-three cases.

This conclusion was accepted world-wide. Jenner went into enormous detail and made medical history for which all of us today must give sincere thanks.

Very gradually, after many investigations by the College of Physicians, his discovery was hailed from the rooftops. It is to Jenner's eternal credit that although he could have now made himself into a very wealthy man, the idea simply never entered his head. His discovery was his gift to the world.

In 1811 he became ill himself and upon his recovery went to London. In 1813 Oxford conferred upon him the degree of MD. He was in London again for three months in 1814 where he met allied sovereigns, the King of Prussia and the Czar. He then returned to Cheltenham, where his wife died in 1815. After that, probably with some of his brilliant spark now diminished with her death, he went back to his roots. Jenner spent the remainder of his life at Berkeley. On 26th January 1823, he died after suffering a fit. He was buried in the chancel of his parish church.

This man's life saved that of countless millions of every race and colour. He was, without a doubt, a dedicated genius and had the courage of his convictions at all times. Today in Berkeley, there is a fascinating museum dedicated to his wonderful life.

This small town, seemingly workaday now, throbs with the history of England and the health of the world. Of all who have lived there, without the shadow of a doubt, Edward Jenner had to be the most famous. Let us all give thanks for his being.

Charfield

<svg><rect/></svg>

Like so many small places of habitation, Charfield was considered too minute and trivial to warrant its own entry in the Domesday Book. There is a very brief mention under the Hundred of Grumbalds Ash with the bald statement that forty families lived there. Much later on, as the centuries passed, another historical record mentions a rector whose stipend was £40.00 per year and that is all.

First of all, there was the usual highly confusing problem of the place's name. Variations ranged from Cirvelde, Vertfieldf, Cherield and Cherefend before it settled down as that which we know it today. In the Old English, 'cect' is held to mean rough ground while 'cearr' indicates a bend or turn.

For many centuries Charfield simply drifted down the years in a peaceful manner and rural harmony until about 1608 when the rot set in. By then the village had two clothiers, ten weavers and thirty-one able-bodied workers. All of these people innocently combined to bring great trouble upon the village through water.

There were a number of weaving mills as Gloucestershire was

most suitable for cloth making but the great problem arose about powering these mills. At this time there were no static or any other kinds of engines such as steam; all possible power had to come through water and the water wheel and it was this use which raised the gremlins' heads.

One water wheel was of fifty hp and needed X amount of water to make the wheel turn satisfactorily. Without this the mill would grind to a halt. Profits would be lost and men laid off work. In turn this would have a domino result and affect all of the village's economy.

The mills at the top of the hill considered they had first call upon the available water while those farther down accused them of pure theft by 'stealing' their vital water. Matters even became ugly on a number of occasions, yet for those even lower down, there was often the feast or famine situation. Even when they did have the precious water, in the winter it became too much and they would flood. The whole business of coping with and utilising this water became rather a hit and miss affair until the advent of the steam engine. Once this was invented and installed, ruffled industrial feathers were able to flatten and allow Charfield to sink back into its rural obscurity.

It seems cruelly ironic that the dreadful disaster which was to happen and shake the village to its foundations, would also be brought about by – water and a steam engine.

It took place on the 13th October 1928 at Charfield railway station. The night had been clear with just a little mist rising from the surrounding fields. The railway line was always very busy with traffic between Gloucester and Bristol and was used by the Great Western Railway as well as the London, Midland and Scottish Railway Companies.

There were four trains involved, all running fairly close together. A Midlands goods' train from Birmingham to Bristol, a Great Western goods from Wolverhampton to Bristol, an LMS parcel train from Leicester to Bristol and, most important of all, a midnight mail from Leeds to Bristol.

A very careful watch was being kept on these trains' movements. The Birmingham goods was shunted at Charfield and the Wolverhampton goods at Berkeley Road. This was to clear the line for the parcel train which happened to be a fast one. This train passed so the signalman at Charfield rang Control to ask whether to forward the other two goods' trains. The Birmingham one was told to go forward from Charfield but, before he left, the tragedy was set in place.

This train drew into Charfield station and spent five minutes taking on water which the signalman had never expected. He had considered he could move both trains and had even accepted that from Berkeley Road which was already on its way. If both of these trains had gone, the Leeds mail would have been delayed. With great reluctance, the signalman realised he would have to shunt the Great Western goods back into a safe lay-by just as soon as it arrived.

A huge part of this disaster in the making lay in the signalling system of that time. The signal to start at Berkeley Road could not be passed until the train activated a release treadle at Charfield.

At 05.13 hours in the morning, the Great Western goods arrived and, as it passed, the signalman shouted to both the driver and the guard that they *must* go into a refuge siding. By then, the train had passed the release treadle so the vital 'Train Out Of Section' was sent back to the Berkeley Road junction.

Already the mail was very close and exactly one minute after the Great Western goods arrived, the express was accepted and terrible death lay only seconds away. The express was moving at sixty miles per hour and the signalman was horrified to grasp that the goods could not clear before the express arrived.

The procedures then in force were so slow and now there was even an empty wagon train approaching Charfield. The signalman saw the express approaching, going flat out and through all of his signals. He was powerless to do anything but watch in disbelieving horror as the 4-4-0 engine number 714, with its eight wooden carriages, charged to destruction.

These wooden carriages were lethal on impact and, what made it all worse, was the fact they were lit by gas with naked flames; a horrifically lethal combination.

The engine hit the wagons of the Great Western first then ricocheted into the up-goods. The carriages reared up and crashed into the over road bridge. The wooden coaches smashed into many pieces with lethal splinters going everywhere and piled into a crazy heap – inside of which were many people. The gas exploded and hungrily pounced upon all this combustible wood and there was virtually a fireball. It has been calculated that inside this horror were between fifty to sixty people.

The quiet little village was abruptly awakened with the appalling noise of the collision. They rushed from their homes, unable to believe their aghast eyes at the tangle of railway wreckage, the horrific flames and trapped passengers waving and screaming for help as the flames began to consume them. They tried but there was little they could do except watch in horror.

Many bodies were later taken to the Railway Tavern where the landlord, Charlie Olds, transformed his pub into a temporary mortuary. Others were taken into cottages until medical help and the police arrived which, with the latter, was rapid as there was a police station to hand.

Guard Johnson was incinerated and could only be identified by his silver buttons. There was no DNA test available then and the bodies were difficult to identify. Two were very badly burned and they appeared to be those of children. Henry Haines, a porter, stated later he remembered seeing them at Gloucester but had they got on the train then or were they, like all children excited by the journey and only looking out of the window?

What happened next has left a permanent question mark over Charfield. No one ever came forward to claim the children's bodies. It is thought their name was that of Saunders because a small, charred item of clothing was found with this nametag attached.

But who were they and who had put them on the express and from which station? Those of limited income would hardly travel on an express; their train trips would be confined to cheap day outings. Who was waiting to take them off the train at Bristol? When children go missing there is always an uproar but not with these two and the mystery deepened. Some held they were not children at all but, if not, people of limited stature would have been even more noticed.

Not long afterwards a lady dressed entirely in black came upon the scene at Churchend, Charfield where there is a memorial to the dead erected by the LMS Railway Company.

This lady always appeared down this narrow, not very well-known lane, in a chauffeur-driven limousine; a vehicle only the rich could then afford. The ordinary man was unable to aspire to anything more than the humble cycle. A car of any kind would have stood out let alone a rich person's vehicle.

She was always expensively dressed but her features could never be seen because of a thick, black veil. The lady would alight from her limousine but utter not one word to anyone including her chauffeur. She would go into the churchyard and head for the memorial. After quite a time she would reappear and be driven away.

None of the villagers attempted to speak to her. They respected her very obvious need for privacy and anonymity. A long talk with one of Charfield's senior residents today gives no fresh clues either. The gentleman distinctly remembers the 'Lady in black' as he saw her on nearly every visit. He was a young boy driving a pony and trap delivering milk and has never forgotten these visits which were two or three times a year. He described the 'Lady in black' as being well set up, definitely a lady of the upper class. She was not small but of fairly mature years and he thought she might have had a frail stature. These strange visits were regular from 1929 until the 'fifties.

Who was she? Did she come to mourn the mysterious children? Were they from her family and, if so, which? Why this total secrecy?

Many years later in 1937, in a totally unrelated court case, a female called Alice Mary Desborough claimed she had been a passenger on the ill-fated express and that the two unknown, small bodies were indeed those of children and they had belonged to her brother. If this is so, why had she taken so many years to speak out?

Why such great secrecy in the first place? Where did the 'Lady in black' fit in to the puzzle? Was someone, for a very unknown reason, wanting these children to disappear into thin air and the train disaster simply expedited this desire? Was their death somehow tied in with an inheritance? Is it possible that there are papers, hidden away in some family, which could throw light upon this enigma but for peculiar reasons, they are still kept hidden even in this twenty-first century?

It is unlikely we will ever have the answers now and the village of Charfield will always have to carry this mystery with its name.

Charlton

Charlton was a very old, historical village typical of so many others in England but it was ruthlessly slaughtered in the twentieth century – for nothing. It did not have its own entry in Domesday book just because it was so tiny, It came under the Hundred of Henbury where it has but a simple mention.

In 1093 the Bishop of Worcester, called Wulfstan, endowed the Monastery at Westbury on Trym and there is a mention made of 2.5 hides of land in Ceorlatune which were given to this Monastery with some in Wice.

Early Charlton had a variety of names which include Cerletone, Cherleton, Chorlton and Charleton to name but a few. There is a later mention in Ecclesiastical records of one hide of land at Charlton with three men and it is thought this was for tithes purposes.

The land division of a Hundred was that used under the old manorial system because nothing would be enclosed until the eighteenth century, so the land was divided into strips of half or one acre. Every peasant, and certainly his lord of the manor, owned a variety of these strips which were often hopelessly scattered about. It all depended upon the actual wealth of the lord in question though thirty strips usually made one holding.

All of these early 'farms' revolved around the lord and each very much depended upon the other in a rough and ready manner. Charlton would have been a pure farming community. Not only would it have had its small manor – somewhere – but there would also be the farms and cottages scattered between them. It had excellent soil and was agriculturally rich even for those days.

Much later, in 1787, Charlton had a sudden rush of blood to its head with a short burst of fame. It was chosen as the place where George Winter's new experiment was to take place. This was to introduce a new and different kind of plough which was fitted with a drill for seed sowing.

This was a huge innovation at that time. Instead of the laborious and often hit-and-miss method of broadcasting seed from the moving hand, this new way gave neat drilled rows which became so much easier to weed and hoe. The crops which were produced were much in advance as they gave a greater yield.

There is another mention of Charlton in 1792 when Charlton Hamlet and tything was contained to about 1,000 acres, annexed to the manor of Westbury. The principal owners were Fiennes Trotman and the families of Teast, Harford and Powell. The Stokes family did not do so bad either.

In the census of 1801 Charlton had exactly ninety-nine inhabitants but halfway through that century this figure had increased considerably. It is easy to imagine the villagers must have considered their way of life as sacrosanct. It suited them nicely. What happened though became a total disgrace to South Gloucestershire.

Charlton was only ever a little village, probably not much above hamlet size. It had a little church, a small chapel and a pub called The Carpenters Arms. There was a general stores cum post office and that was it. There were the farms and cottages, a duck pond and a common. What Charlton also had was a tight-knit community spirit.

In the early twentieth century though an ugly dragon lifted its threatening head, although this was not recognised initially and even for many years. The British and Colonial Aeroplane Company was founded in Bristol and a factory was set up at the old bus depot at Filton.

Aeroplanes need space though – lots of it too; even the archaic string bag early planes of those long ago days. The villagers were still unperturbed. Some of their men folk worked at the Filton factory which gave them better money than with farming.

There was a lot of activity in World War I but afterwards came the lean years of the 'twenties. World War II was a very different kettle of fish indeed. This was the civilian's war. Air raid shelters now appeared at Charlton with the increased population figures because of 'the works' as they were called.

Charlton did not escape Hitler's bombers either. The village was vulnerable as it was so near to Filton runway and a number of bombs fell upon it. One man was away during a raid and returned to find his whole family had taken cover in an underground shelter. This had received a direct hit from a 500lb bomb and he was the sole survivor.

Events were also 'happening' at the works but at first in total secrecy. Then rumours started to grow. In 1943 a committee was formed with a brief to consider civil aircraft for when the war did end. This was certainly positive thinking but it was doomed to travel the wrong road. All the committee could think about was a giant plane based upon the existing bombers of the times.

This great plane would carry rich people across the Atlantic to America in the lap of luxury.

Also at this time, admittedly in the greatest of security and secrecy, Frank Whittle, later to be knighted, had already tested his revolutionary jet engine from his Power Jet workshops in Leicestershire. It is true a German had been credited with the jet's invention but it was Frank Whittle who refined the idea and made it workable.

Surely there were people in The Establishment who must have had some clues about this jet? Surely they could recognise its potential? Surely they could see that the day and age of the piston and turbo engine would soon be relegated with that of the dinosaur?

The blinkered committee planned for the future with a giant plane whose interior would be as luxurious as that of an ocean liner. It would be first class only. Humble Joe Bloggs, his missus and family did not enter their equation at all.

It was decided to call the plane the Brabazon after Lord Brabazon of Tara. She would have a gross weight of 100 tons. To get this monster into the air there would be eight colossal engines, coupled in pairs. It would have a maximum take-off weight of 129 tons yet its cruising speed would only be a pathetic 160 miles per hour.

To make matters worse, it came out that such a giant plane would need an equally huge hangar covering 7.5 acres. There was also the question of a very long runaway.

Charming and innocent little Charlton stood slap bang in the way. A village which had stood for countless centuries and also one with very rich farming lands. Then the bombshell exploded. Charlton would have to go.

This shattering announcement was made from the House of Lords that the village, the roads and all of the people's houses were to be bulldozed into the ground. There was a blaze of angry publicity. The people were enraged and rightly so. Many wept openly and not just females either. This was their happy home. This was their village. What about *their* rights?

Did any of this cut ice? Not one particle. Charlton stood in the way of progress. The people of Charlton were – very sorry and all that – expendable. Naturally, there would be some compensation. A new village was blithely promised but 'Go!' the people of Charlton must.

The villagers clung miserably to their beloved Charlton to no avail. They must leave and would be rehoused in Patchway. This was madness. They were country people and not urbanites. The transition would be too great. The final few days in their wonderful village was agony but already concrete was being poured for the extended runway.

With breaking hearts they were forced to move and, in their distress, many left objects through forgetfulness. In a panic they rushed back to their cottages the next day but everything had 'vanished'.

The treatment these villagers suffered can only be classed as utterly despicable.

But what about the wonder plane, the Brabazon, the instigator of all this heartbreak and uproar? She was already twenty-seven months late in making her maiden flight. On the 4th September 1949, Bill Pegg, the Chief Test Pilot, took off and flew the giant plane – despite it already being branded obsolete.

Work started though on a Brabazon Mark II which was designed to have four 7,000 hp turbo prop engines but this plane's wing design fell short of requirements. It was also discovered that the expected fatigue life of this aircraft would be a mere 5,000 flying hours. So the decision was made to consign both planes to the scrap heap at the cost of three million pounds, at 'forties' valuation, a vast sum of money.

What is left of pretty, little Charlton today? A tiny stretch of Catbrain Lane, a short portion of Charlton Road and a miniscule part of Charlton Common. A charming little village which had stood for well over one thousand years was viciously destroyed. A piece of old England had gone forever leaving behind broken-hearted families, just ordinary people and consequently, powerless ones. People whose families had lived in Charlton village for countless generations. Was anyone ever held accountable? If not, why not?

Chedworth

That remarkable road which we call the A429 cuts right across the heart of England, running from the southwest to the northeast, hardly deviating except for the modern sections. It runs up and downhill, devastatingly accurate, scything across rich farmlands with glorious views in parts yet how many drivers realise they are passing through a wonderful portion of England's history? The Roman Road the Fosse is over 2,000 years old yet still serves the great god motor car.

About 1.5 miles due west lies the village of Chedworth, unknown to so many drivers and their passengers, yet this spot echoes our history. This place was in the Hundred of Rapsgate and had fifteen old names, two of which are Ceddanwryde and Cheddewrda. It is thought they all refer to Cedda's enclosure as, in the Old English, this is what the word is taken to mean.

Somewhere around the second century after Christ, a villa was built by a Roman who must have been fairly rich. What he was doing in Albion, in the first place, we have no idea. By and large, the sun-loving Romans, especially those of wealth, would have their homes where sunshine was guaranteed. Perhaps he held some important position; there is even the chance he saw nothing wrong with our climate because Romans, as a race, knew exactly how to look after their creature comforts in their private homes.

This Roman had to be of the self-sufficiency brigade because it is certain there was a fulling mill present. (Fulling – the process of cleansing, shrinking, and thickening cloth by moisture, heat, and pressure.) There were, as well, drying vats and carding combs, found centuries later. Nearby is a hill from which the vital fuller's earth could be obtained. No Roman worth his patrician nose would ever turn away the chance to make money by honest trade.

There would also have been considerable agriculture because such a huge villa would have had many mouths to feed: not just the Roman's family and their guests but the huge array of slaves they would have kept to keep the wheels running smoothly.

With the knowledge of the fulling mill this also tells us the Roman must have had his own sheep. Wolves still prevailed then, which meant extra guards for these animals and their general husbandry.

Inscriptions have been found which seem to point to the fact this family were Christian. They would then probably fall within the category of the Romano-British: purebred Romans who might never have seen Rome but who still considered Rome, and its way of life, the only way to live. It is highly unlikely they would take kindly to being called British.

We do know there were other Romano-British sites in this particular region. There was also a well used salt trail not far away which traversed the Cotswolds in general. Salt was so vital for life, not just for normal eating but for preserving. No fridge freezers in those days!

Gradually these people did die out or became assimilated into general society through intermarriages. Certainly once the Legions had departed after their 400 years of occupation, the field was wide open for the Saxons and other land-hungry races.

By this time, Chedworth would have had well tilled land which was highly valuable for crops and animals. A rich land, but the Saxons came from a different culture and they had their own ideas of living.

England sank into gloom for many decades and slowly the villa would have been left as the last remnants of the family died. It would have become a prey to wind, weather, Nature and vandals because the latter have always been with us. So one day the villa would have vanished completely both from sight and memory.

We know there was a donation by Ealdred who was an under king of the Hwicce when they paid tribute to Mercia. This was roughly in the third quarter of the eighth century when a gift of 'Fifteen cassati at Ceddanwryde in terra montana' was given but by whom and to whom? By now the name roughly translates to Chedworth on the Wolds.

Then came William with his mighty Normans. It is known William did ride over this part of his newly acquired territory but going to and where from we have no idea. His Domesday survey does give us a few more clues.

The entry for Chedworth says it was held by Wulfward which is a Saxon name. There were fifteen hides of woodland and open meadows. There were seven ploughs in the whole lordship before the 1086 survey which included sixteen villagers, three smallholders and six ploughs. Strangely enough no slaves or servie are mentioned.

It was no poor little place either, even then, because there were three mills in existence. William's clerks calculated they were worth 14/2 – a sum impossible to decimalise after so many centuries. There was a toll on the salt which went to the hall. The sheriff also added eight villagers and three smallholders with four ploughs.

Although slavery had, strictly speaking, been abolished, the word servie was nothing but a fancy disguise for people still in bondage. It is out of the question to think Chedworth had none. Were they hidden at the time of the survey and, if so, why? A tantalising question.

We also know that nearby Coin St Denis, which was in the Hundred of Deerhurst, was given by the King to the Abbey of St Dennis, Paris in 1069.

By then, no one would have known, or even cared, about a long-lost Roman villa. William was far too busy trying to find out what his new country was worth to him. At the same time, he had to keep a beady eye on the dispossessed Britons who bubbled with resentment. There were also his new barons to watch in case they developed ideas above their station in life.

William himself had started to get fat and heavy and his health was not what it might have been, so, adding up all these problems, is it any wonder his temper could be tetchy at times?

For many centuries the villa remained hidden. Kings lived and died, each with their own foibles. Gradually the races mixed and settled down to make the English. There were still odd outbursts but, by and large, people were reasonably quiet.

It is thought the manor house was built in mediaeval times though it might have been tampered with as a result of various owners' ideas. It is possible it once had three stories and not two. At one stage, not all that far away, was a preceptory of the Knights Hospitaliers from Quenington but very little appears in the old records about this.

St Andrew's church, set against a hill slope, was probably of the Norman period because they were passionate church builders. Later generations changed this structure, here and there and the reason again is unknown.

At the dissolution, Henry VIII seized so much and the abbey leased the manor in two separate parts to Hugh Westwood of Chedworth. He became the founder of Northleach Grammar School as well as the builder of Almshouses at Bibury.

In 1826 Cobbet was busily engaged upon his rural rides. He came to this part of the Cotswolds and hated the place. The stunning views meant nothing to him, which is understandable. He was really only interested in how many crops could be grown to fill empty bellies.

He is reputed to have said, "The soil is what is called *stone brash*, with a reddish earth mixed with bits of brash on top. The soil is shallow and the fields are even divided with this brash. One can look, for mile after mile, and not see any trees. This is a sort of country having less to please the eye than any other

I have seen." Rather a damning verdict and not just Cobbet's alone.

Sydney Smith labelled it a land of stone and sorrow. It appears each critic was glad to leave this part of the Cotswolds well behind his horse. Cobbet did admit there were some fertile wolds and dells with one or two pretty meadows but, by and large, it is obvious this area was not his cup of tea.

In that same century a great discovery was made by a gamekeeper in 1864. He had lost his ferret and started to dig down a rabbit hole to rescue it. In the process he came across some Tesseraer.

By great good fortune he recognised it for what it was and immediately suspected there must be something more under the earth. The Earl of Eldon, at his own expense, had everything excavated then in 1865 he also provided a museum to show off the wonderful artefacts which had been discovered. Later on in the twentieth century, this became a home and the old Roman villa, the property of the National Trust.

The historians consider the rediscovered villa was built in three or even four bursts. In the first half of the second century it consisted of three separate ranges, a half-timbered building on the south, a main western block and a small bath suite which would have faced north: the whole situated at the head of a wooden valley.

In the early third century wings had been added to the west and south. It is agreed the final shape, though not finished until the fourth century, ended up the most magnificent villa with a covered veranda which joined all the buildings together.

At the same time this made a delightful courtyard and inner garden. The Romans adored their gardens and were especially fond of lilies, violets, myrtle and roses. They considered the simple dog rose contained a cure for hydrophobia.

They grew ivy extensively, trailing it around posts and tree trunks. They would also insist upon a hortus for growing fruit trees and vegetables. Many of our now familiar fruits such as pears and cherries come to us from Roman introduction. It is considered they were also responsible for bringing in and growing the humble carrot as well as peas, asparagus, lettuce, radish, turnip and marrows.

The whole of this villa would have been connected with the splendid road to Corinium, today's Cirencester, always an important town both for the old British as well as the Romans.

There is one school of thought which holds that all the late fourth-century additions indicated a change of use for this villa. If so, for what? A new ritual? Did it then revert back to a humble farmhouse? What really happened to those who lived there? Who were they? It is frustrating to have learned so much, then grind to a halt.

It is obvious the rot set in with the advancing, aggressive Saxons who were far more interested in the conquest of land than a mere Roman villa, so this lovely place sank back into gloom and total obscurity until rediscovered in the mid-nineteenth century. Now we can go and see it for ourselves and be highly respectful to what our distant ancestors managed to accomplish without any of our modern electronic gadgets. Does this mean they were better than us? A thought-provoking question surely?

Cirencester

Throughout its long existence, Cirencester has had many names. At one count thirty-three were found and there are probably even more if dialect is taken into account. They vary enormously from some which we can recognise like Syrencestre and Durocornovio to the Welsh Kaer Vudei. This latter name comes from the Welsh, to churn, which hints heavily that the two words mean a fort of the churn but a churn of what? Now that we do not know.

Other variations include the word korn which, freely translated, means simply horn and we have, for example, Cornwall or the horn of the land which is a very good description for that part of the country.

Even famous Dyer Street, so called because that was where all the cloth dyers habituated, was once known as Chepynstret. The town was the Roman Corinium and many people today still affectionately call it that. They consider it was the Romans who established the town.

They did not. The Dubonii were there first and it was in this area they minted their own quite good coins. They considered this town the capital for their tribal area although the West Midlands tribe of the Cornovii were not above calling it 'theirs' which never sat well with the Dubonii.

There is a very early history by John Milton which was written from deductions by Geoffrey of Monmouth. It was his opinion that a leader called Dunwallo, about 474BC, was reputed to be an overall King.

We do not have one shred of proof and, knowing the ancient tribes, this was highly unlikely. They were much too busy fighting each other to come together under one King. Geoffrey has never been considered the best of historians so what he says must be taken with an enormous amount of salt.

The natural, instinctive aggression of the early tribes raised even more question marks. Britain, prior to the Romans, was strictly divided into tribal territories and there was nothing the tribes adored more than a good fight. War was a delight to them. An entertaining sport and occupation. Not that which arose from natural hatred.

Cirencester's early history was one of ups and downs. First it was a British town though this would not fit in with the Romans' notion of one. It was probably nothing but a fairly large settlement with boundary walls, dykes and ramparts. There would be general defences and space for all of the tribe's animals.

When the Romans arrived they would have seen the town's

potential. They probably grinned at the Britons idea of a 'town' and promptly set to work to sort out what they could do with this pathetic British affair. It is thought the town was founded in the time of the emperor Claudius and was first of all a Roman station. Two tombs have been found dating from about AD100 and were of cavalrymen.

Many villas sprang up in the region, their construction encouraged by roads. One historian quotes, "Beyond doubt, rich men must have been as common as weeds around Corinium during the Roman age."

Indeed it was a flourishing town with agriculture the main source of wealth because there were weekly, and sometimes monthly markets, It was considered a capital for this part of the country and this seems to have lasted well to the end of the fourth century.

After the Romans departed from their 400 years' occupation the town started to go to the dogs. The whole country fell into a state of flux because after so long an occupation, many of the Britons had forgotten how to fight.

It did not take them long though to realise they had better get their ability back because waiting in the wings were other land-hungry invaders, all of whom fancied making Britain theirs. They were the Saxons, nobody's pushover either.

In 577 a tremendously important battle took place in which King Ceawlin of the Saxons thrashed three British Kings at the battle of Deorham and took the three towns of Gloucester, Bath and Cirencester. The British Kings were Coinmail, Farinmail and Condidan. They were all good fighters and combined to face the Saxons but, as always before, they and their men went in for far too much prancing and shouting beforehand. When the Saxons did fight the Britons were half exhausted and Ceawlin's Saxon guile and disciplined soldiers did the rest.

These Saxons were pagans and they destroyed all evidence of Christianity. This was not restored until after Penda's death in 655. In 628 Penda of Mercia, the last of the heathen Kings, appeared at Cirencester and made a treaty with the West Saxons and married his sister to Coinwalch, their Prince. It must have been a bit of a rocky marriage because Coinwalch repudiated his wife. Penda then descended again like a ton of bricks and annexed all of the area to that of Mercia. Some historians think it was at this time the town was abandoned for the time being. It was Penda's son Peada, a Christian, who brought some life back to the town before he was murdered and died from poison. The next King was Wulfhere, another pagan, but one who became a Christian.

There was a gentle lull for the town for about 250 years, then Guthram and his Danes appeared about 878. They were allowed to encamp outside the town. These Danes had been beaten by Alfred and forced to make their peace with him but Cirencester was not Alfred. It was, instead, fair game.

They stayed for about a year which obviously made the town's inhabitants decidedly nervous and uneasy. There is a small, unproven tale which says Guthram captured many sparrows. He tied combustible material to their feet and let them loose. They flew into Cirencester, landed on the roofs and set the town ablaze. This ploy, if true, gave Cirencester the nickname of Sparrow Town for a short while.

One of the next great events was the arrival of Knut, or Canute, as we call him. He held an important general council at Easter in Cirencester upon his return from Denmark. He made two men into outlaws for very bad behaviour and they were lucky not to lose their heads.

Canute built a small castle but this was demolished by Stephen somewhere around 1141 but ten years before this there was a second prosperous time. It was in 1131 that Henry I built an Augustinian abbey which became very wealthy and which owned large tracts of the County and many valuable sheep. By the fourteenth century, the abbots owned and stored 20,000 bales of wool in their buildings, This power even increased when Richard I sold both the manor and the town to the abbey for

£100 plus a rent of £30 a year, quite a handsome bargain then. This great abbey did not survive the Dissolution because Henry VIII sold on to Roger Bassinge on the stated condition that the buildings be demolished. All that remains now is the hospital gate.

The town however did prosper very well because it had one of the largest wool markets in the country. This wealth accounts for its truly magnificent church whose tower forms a landmark for a considerable distance around. It was started in about 1400 and it was roughly at this time that the two-storied South Porch, facing the Market Square, was also built. For quite a while the upper storey was used as the Town Hall.

In 1515 there were alterations to the twelfth-century nave when it was replaced by the present one. The church stands in the place where stalls are held on one day in the week and cars have to give way. Opposite the church is an old inn called the King's Inn. The story goes that the very first fighting of the Civil wars started there in 1642.

During 1700, Defoe visited the town and wrote admiringly of it, commenting how full it was of rich clothiers and what a huge trade it did in wool. That though did not last because there became a lessening demand for Cotswold wool so this trade declined. It was the old story; lack of water for mechanisation of the mills. When steam power did arrive coal was not easy to get as the main railway from London to Gloucester by-passed the town.

So slowly the rot set in but there was another third burst of prosperity with the introduction of many light industries to the town. This was all done thoughtfully so none of the town's ancient charm was lost.

Today Cirencester, still affectionately called Corinium by some, retains not just its old world charm but many connections with its ancient past. The museum has splendid examples of Roman mosaics and there is a superb amphitheatre. There are also ancient lock-ups which appeared in the eighteenth century. They usually had a domed roof which gave them the nickname of 'round houses' or 'dumpling houses', rather unique to the County.

For visitors with cars it can be a nightmare to park. A lot of the streets are one-way and it is better to park outside and walk in. For the disabled there are some special bays in the Market Square. There is certainly a huge amount to see and take in because Cirencester, or if you prefer it, Corinium, bristles with our history and the town is a real gem.

The Crossed Hands

The high land which makes today's A46 road has always been a popular place going way back into the mists of time. It is a natural communications route and would have been used by the early tribal people, long before Rome cast her greedy eyes upon this land.

Many artefacts have been found, scattered here and there, dug up by some farmer's plough or enterprising archaeologist, which proves this fact. When the Romans did arrive, it was land occupied by the Dubonii tribe.

There are three Sodburys each with a collection of names and perhaps that most applicable to this high land was Soppa's place. Today's Old Sodbury had a huge range of names with some weird spellings but who Soppa was, we have no idea.

It is doubtful the Romans leaned much from the British except that they held the Druids in the highest esteem. They did learn that the Dubonii could and would fight. Apart from this though, each side was inclined to despise the other. What the Britons did admire though was that at which Romans truly excelled; their marvellously, straight roads which surmounted nearly all obstacles.

From Old Sodbury the track ran straight up the hill very steeply. At the top, on the edge of the natural escarpment, the Romans became extremely busy.

The main Roman artery was the Fosse Way, sometimes also called the Akerman Street. This ran from Bath direct to Cirencester. After their four centuries of occupation the Romans departed and their fine roads fell into disrepair, their villas hidden after being vandalised by newcomers, then taken over by wind and weather.

Just before the Conquest, the area was in the Hundred of Grumbald's Ash and held by a son of Algar called Brictric. This son was either arrogant or a trifle on the thick side. Perhaps, though, he just did not understand females.

The Lady Matilda fancied him but Brictric foolishly scorned her hand. Like all of her gender, what she lacked in muscle power she more than made up for with guile and the patience for revenge. She eventually married William I and promptly sorted Brictric out with a vengeance. He lost the whole of his vast estate and was lucky not to lose his head as well.

Domesday tells us that Old Sodbury had twelve villeins, four bordars, five plough tillages and eighteen servie. This is a huge number for such a small place. The area then descended through inheritance and matrimony until it eventually ended up belonging to Anne, the sister of Henry Beauchamp, Duke of Warwick.

She married Richard Nevil who was killed at Barnet Field and who had made the serious error of backing the wrong house, that of Lancaster, in the Yorkist wars. It is recorded that his widow became 'obnoxious' to the monarch. Henry VII had few scruples under normal circumstances and he bullied the lady very badly.

She had no option but to settle the greater part of her inheritance upon him and his heirs. The king also levied a heavy fine upon her.

Henry VIII gave the manor to Sir John Walsh who had been his champion. It was bought during the reign of James I, then slowly passed down to Winchcome-Henry Harley.

By now it is pretty certain this was an insignificant area, much tinier and of less importance than its bustling neighbour Chipping

Sodbury. All it really had to show was its track climbing up the hill to the well-worn trail above the escarpment.

The roads, such as they were, now left much to be desired but finally some effort was made to tame them again. That along the top of the rise became a Turnpike Road so received the maximum attention.

With the advent of the stagecoach, a degree of smoothness for horses and coach wheels became vital. Coaches became a common sight. There was even some talk of making a new road that would connect the part known as the Cross Hands with Tormarton.

How did the name Cross Hands originate? We have no idea. It is most likely connected with the road system and the natural crossing point for all travellers; a 'cross roads' name which simply grew. We do know there was a farm called the Cross Hands which, at one time, also held the Petty Sessional Court also called the Magistrates Court.

It's reasonable to accept this general name of something 'crossing' then a remarkable discovery was made. In 1820 an old coin was found at the site of today's Cross hands Hotel; not just any old coin either. It depicted a bust with two right hands crossed in a handshake. There was a small, hard-to-read inscription but it was the two crossed hands which aroused the greatest interest.

The coin was dated from 267AD and now it is in a Bristol museum. It is nice and romantic to think it is this coin which gives us the names Crossed Hands but there is very little tangible evidence, and few probable facts to substantiate this.

During the reign of George IV a new road was built to the top of the hill. The original was more direct but far too steep for the comfort of man or beast. This resulted in a turnpike road between the Cross Hands and Yate.

The private residence known as the Cross Hands was rebuilt. For a very short space of time it might have been an inn until the Plough took over this function. Once again the building reverted to a private home.

What do we have today? We have the large Cross Hands Hotel which stands right at the crossroads and which dominates the area. It stands four square and proud, guarded by an enormous tree.

It is a popular hotel with a number of bars and eating rooms. If you go there to drink or dine, do not forget the site is incredibly ancient as the old Crossed Hands' coin shows us. History lived at the Crossed Hands.

Dursley

It is reasonably certain that the area of today's Dursley has always been favoured even by very early man. Prior to Christ, we know that man lived in his encampment at nearby Uley because high land made it a perfect defensive position. The Romans also would appreciate such an area. Even without a station there they would certainly have had regular patrols to keep an ever-watchful eye upon the Dubonii who did not take all that kindly to their occupation.

There were eighteen old names for Dursley which include Dersilege, Dursseley and Deusley. These are considered to come from the old English and translate to Deorsige's clearing.

Usually the two great historians, Rudder and Atkyns in their remarkable histories of Gloucestershire, agree with each other but in Dursley's case there is a slight contretemps. Atkyns says the word of dur is the old British for water and leay means simply a pasture ground. Rudder states the name for the tiny town was Ewelm which relates to the head of a spring and that it is the word dwr which signifies the water. He says the letter 's' was only added to make the general name more agreeable. It is likely both are correct depending upon the period of their use and by which race of people, British, Saxon or Norman.

Dursley lies in the Hundred of Berkeley and has always had

some kind of market for centuries. It is one of five ancient Boroughs of the County and has always been considered quite important although all criminals of the area were always taken to Berkeley to be tried and executed.

The actual manor of Berkeley was given to Roger de Berkeley by William I with three hides of land. Not really a vast amount either, so was William being a bit parsimonious for once or just his usual cautious self? It was this Roger de Berkeley who became the founder of the monastery at Kingswood and the old records state he was certified upon an aid. This meant a payment from a feudal lord, a little bit like a modern backhander for marrying the king's daughter, so he also held one hide at Dursley. He was allowed to levy scutage to wage war against Scotland which certified six knights' fees and half which were held of the honour of Dursley. It was a very expensive business even in those days to provide and equip one knight let alone six though the half remains an intriguing mystery. Scutage, or escutage, was the duty imposed on a tenant of accompany his lord to war for forty days, sending a substitute or paying a sum of money instead.

Dursley continued to be in this family's ownership until the reign of Edward IV. It went out of the Berkeleys hands because of the marriage of Maud to Robert de Cantelupe. In turn, their daughter married Thomas Wekys so the Wekys became the Dursley family of consequence for many years. Then another Robert Wekys sold the whole lot to the Estcourts and we can only guess he was in dire need of hard cash or was made such a magnificent offer he simply could not refuse. The Earl of Berkeley is always Viscount of the place and this title goes to the eldest son of the Berkeley family.

As far as the castle is concerned it is thought this was built sometime during the early part of the fourteenth century. Both of the great historians in their books are inclined to be rather scathing about this castle's construction. One of them says it was built of 'towse stone which was full of holes and pores like pumice'. It appears this came from a fossil substance found in plenty in the Parish and was so soft it could easily be cut into blocks and when it had dried it hardened. Certainly such an obviously soft stone could not stand against the elements like more solid castles constructed from blocks of naturally hard stone like granite.

Dursley Castle gradually fell into decay and was taken down. Some of the materials were then used in building a manor house at Dodington by a Robert Wekys who was then the lord of both Dursley and Dodington.

The castle was reputed to have had a good moat according to one historian but another argues the building was not a proper castle at all. He says it was nothing but a glorified manor house which was castellated and had a 'dytch' around it. It was held to be somewhere near to the upper and lower castle fields about a quarter of a mile northwest of the town centre.

It was Dursley who gave England Edward Fox, who became the bishop of Hereford and did much to help in the reformation. It was he who introduced Cranmer to King Henry VIII.

Dursley has not been without other characters also. One was called William Hopkins who turned out to be nothing but a sheer genius. Until his health deteriorated in his early forties, he was a journeyman miller. It is known he could barely read or write and his knowledge of figures was just enough for him to get by with his work.

Not long after his early retirement as a miller he became interested in music and fancied he could make a violin despite disparaging comments from his peers. It did not take him long to make this instrument and then, with neither help nor hesitation, he taught himself to play. Encouraged, he then made a bass viol which he also learned to play by himself.

Flushed with success, he then built a chamber organ in his master's mill and after much hard work and experimentation, he brought it to perfection. He was clever enough to contrive that the great water wheel of the mill, while performing its ordinary work, would also work the bellows of the organ. At the same time, it would turn a spit with meat on it before the kitchen fire – and all this while the inventor played sacred music! He then built another organ in the Dursley Meeting House which was admired by all and sundry for its fullness, purity and the harmony of its tones. At no time did he receive either help or advice, so with education what might not this genius have invented?

In 1790 a book was published titled *A Provincial Glossary* which dealt with sayings and dialects. It held there were two specific to Dursley. The first was 'As sure as God's in Gloucestershire'. This arose from the number of religious houses in the County which were stated to be double the number and value than anywhere else. The second saying was short and pithy: 'You are a man of Dursley!' It was a highly uncomplimentary way of saying someone had broken his promise. It probably alluded to some ancient and notorious breach of good faith by some unknown and long-forgotten person.

In 1678 Thomas Shakespeare, a weaver, was married in Dursley. Long before this wedding, Shakespeare was a fairly common name for the region. There were Shakespeares all around as well as at Bisley, Beverston and Newington Bagpath. The Hathways or Hathaways were also a family connected with the County and it is thought that when William married his Anne in 1582, he may somehow have upset Stratford friends because he was only eighteen years and she twenty-six, an age imbalance which might not go down at all well with the families in question. It is a positive legend that Shakespeare with his young wife is thought to have taken refuge in the Dursley area until he made his momentous move to London.

This is virtually confirmed by Shakespeare's plays in which he displays a considerable knowledge of the region. In *Henry IV*, Part II, Act V the scene is set in the County at Shallow's house. In the garden, the servant Davy says to Shallow, 'I beseech you, sir, to countenance William Visor of Wincot against Clement Perkes of the hill.' Wincot or Woncot were local dialect names for Woodmancote and the Wolds were commonly known as The Hill.

In *Richard II*, Act II, Scene III, Shakespeare is firm in placing this scene in The Wolds of Gloucestershire. Then Bolingbroke asks North, 'How far is it, my lord, to Berkeley?' North replies he is a stranger to the County and goes on to comment about 'these wild hills and rough uneven ways', all of which show that Shakespeare must have ridden fairly extensively around and about this region.

A few centuries later the situation had improved very little because there were bitter complaints about the roads and their tolls even as late as 1847. From Tetbury to Dursley it cost one old shilling and sixpence for the nine and a half miles journey for a horse and trap; a quite considerable sum then. It was just ten miles from Dursley to Minchinhampton and that meant two whole shillings had to be paid to use the road. Horsley Hill was considered a total disgrace with its ruts and gutters across the road as well as being highly dangerous to man and beast. It was twelve miles from Dursley to Stroud and the charge here was the astronomical one of two shillings and sixpence. The general and common grievance was that the County boasted the highest tolls possible for the worst roads imaginable in the whole of England.

In 1738 the Estcourt family built the distinctive market house in the centre of the town as Dursley was the hub for the whole vale of Berkeley and famous for its butter and cheese markets. Now it is a superb tourist attraction, a splendid example of such architecture.

Like all such towns connected with the Cotswolds, Dursley had its boom years through the clothing industry when a lot of money was made by everyone from clothier down to humble weaver and cottage worker. When this industry declined so too did the well-paying work and many fell upon hard times, especially the ordinary people.

The first census was held in 1801 and the population was

registered as 2,379. Over the various ten-year periods between each census, the figure fluctuated up and down according to the town's good or bad fortunes. At one time it was only just under 3,000 persons and the records state, quite proudly, these totals always included the inmates of the workhouse.

In the summer of 1936 a wedding took place which turned into a most unusual and rare celebration. Stanley Harris married Miss Bray. On that particular day, the groom's parents celebrated their own silver wedding while the groom's paternal grandparents celebrated their golden jubilee in the same church where *they* had been married. It is to be asked what would be the odds of something similar taking place again anywhere in the country?

The modern Dursley has had its share of brisk and busy industry and has, for decades, been the home of the *Gazette* newspaper. It is quite a quaint little town, sitting in a dip and surrounded by woods and hills. Through the gaps in the trees there can be obtained gorgeous views, and, in so many ways, it epitomises the long history of this country from the barrows at nearby Uley, long before Christ, to our twenty-first century. What better accolade can any town want but that?

Dyrham

The sleepy little village of Dyrham has had its day of glory, or notoriety, depending upon whether one was victor or loser.

Ghosts are there which go back to AD577 – but who knows today?

In those days, Britain was certainly not united, even though the Saxons had decided that the wet island was ideal for settlement.

At times, the British had an overall king called Bretwalda, but his power was extremely limited for one simple reason; there were no sports of football and cricket to let off steam. Instead, the Britons of those days did their own thing by the finest sport of all, fighting each other. War was a glory game, a fact King Ceawlin of the Saxons knew well.

He gambled that the argumentative and battling Britons would be too busy attacking each other to take much notice of him. So he invaded. It was crucial for his plans to conquer this part of Britain before moving northwards. With his brother Cutha, Ceawlin was confident before he marched anywhere near to the village. So sure of himself was he that he did not bother to sack Bath, telling his men they would do this later. The Saxons climbed the hill north of Bath and headed unerringly towards the Britons.

Unknown to Ceawlin, frantic political and diplomatic negotiations had been taking place and the three local kings, Coinmail, Conidan and Farinmail had at last been persuaded to see sense. They had dropped any local grievances to turn and face the greater foe – the invading Saxon army of King Ceawlin. However, their united strength made them just a little too cocky for their own good. On the high land above the village of Dyrham to one side, and Hinton on the other, they gathered to face the Saxons.

What they did not take into consideration was the fact that hilltops rarely have water. This was all down below, where they put their horse herds. Fighting, man-to-man, with heavy swords is sweat-making and very thirsty work.

Ceawlin was bright. Although taken aback at the huge force which faced him on the hilltop he did not allow himself to be unduly perturbed. He carefully weighed up the situation while keeping his men back, but compact. The sun shone. The Britons, followed their usual pattern, cavorted backwards and forwards, howling threats and challenges, exhausting themselves before a blow had been struck. Ceawlin kept himself prudently out of range and ignored the Britons' taunts while continuing to weigh up the situation.

He was outnumbered, but his guile exceeded that of the three kings. He knew something the Britons did not know. His knowledge was gained from past experiences and he issued his orders calmly. The Britons had erected two frontal ridges which faced him and behind which they pranced and bellowed, waving their weapons with defiance. Ceawlin's secret was the proven fact that when men fight in battle and go downhill they unerringly curve inwards. He had also worked out that the Britons had no water; everything had to be hauled to the high land from the village below.

He split his men into three and when he considered the Britons had exhausted themselves and were dehydrated, he attacked. The centre line of warriors marched forward with right and left flanks restrained.

It was vicious hand-to-hand fighting but the Saxons were fresher. They breached the first defensive ridge then hurled themselves at the second. It was now the exhausted Britons understood the error of their ways.

They started to break. First a few men, then a handful, then a general rout to retreat to the village below where there was water and fresh mounts. At this moment, Ceawlin released his flank warriors.

They hurtled after the weary Britons and, as Ceawlin well knew, curved inwards towards the bottom of the hill. There they met and the bulk of the retreating Britons were trapped in the circle. All they could do was die.

It is to their credit that the three kings died with their men so the Britons, in this region, were decimated and totally conquered by the guile of the Saxon king.

This great victory gave the Saxons control of Bath. Gloucester and Cirencester but they only ever held control for fifty years.

The whole area north of the River Avon gradually became Mercian by conquest.

Ferries over the Severn

❧⚜❧

Ferries have plied the waters of the mighty River Severn for a good 2,000 years.

And when one considers the flimsy craft of those far-off days, it is reasonable to conjecture how many travellers would have drowned because the Severn is a very unforgiving river.

Aust has had a number of names including Aeustin, Austa, Angst and Augusta. It is thought that today's name came from the 2nd Roman Legion, the Legio Ausgustus. Artefacts have been found which indicate a Roman settlement.

Aust Passage, later to be known as Old Passage to distinguish it from New Passage, has red and grey cliffs which hold incredible, rare fish fossils and were responsible for industrial chemistry.

In the nineteenth century, William Buckland, Dean of Westminster, explored the Aust cliffs. At the same time, a German chemist, Baron Liebig, visited England. They met and went to Aust to dig for fossil bones, some of which crumbled. Upon returning to Germany, the Baron came up with the idea of pulverising bones and guano to make fertiliser, and so started industrial chemistry.

Domesday gives us but a cryptic statement in that Thurstan, son of Rolf, held five hides at Aust.

In the early twelfth century the de Clares were the lords of Tidenham and they granted quittance to the monks at Tintern to use their crossing.

By 1405 great numbers of English and Welsh used the chapel at St Twrog, and crossing the river between Aust and Beachley was very important.

Aust to Beachley is just one mile, but what a hazardous one. The tides run very swiftly and the river can turn rough in minutes.

This fact deterred *Daniel Defoe*, of Robinson Crusoe fame, from crossing in a sailing ship. On 1st September 1839 the ship

The Dispatch went down in mid-channel. Captain Whitechurch was drowned along with his son, nine or ten others, five horse and two carriages. In 1743 Charles Wesley was lucky to escape shipwreck when crossing in wild weather.

In 1825 the Post Office wanted a reliable way to cross with the mails and the New Passage was the preferred route despite the greater length on the water.

From 1827 the St Pierre found herself in competition with larger, faster Old Passage ships, so New and Old fought a commercial war.

Mail coaches were diverted to Old Passage and they, too, formed a company. Stone piers were built and by 1830 Old Passage had won.

In 1845 the South Wales Railway wanted a link and acquired the crossing rights from both Old and New Passages on both sides of the river, but their bridge dreams were doomed. Engineers faced enormous problems. Not only did they have to consider the Severn's enormous power but also its huge tidal rise and fall and uneven riverbed.

From the Aust side there is a great stretch of shallow water and mud which, at low tide, exposes the English Stones, a reef of hard marl. On the west side is a rock shelf called the Lady Beach. Between these is the notorious Shoots, 400 yards wide and 95 feet deep with a 10-knot current. So, by Act of Parliament, bridges were out and tunnels in.

Work also began on a 1,635 feet long pier on the east side which went to a steamer pontoon.

A hotel for passengers to await their crossing provided the height of luxury and even had a small hospital for those who were sea-sick. There was also a rank of terraced cottages for the workers and the ferryboat's captain.

There were three paddle steamers: *The Gem, The Relief* and *The President* and in 1864 a purpose-built ferry *The Christopher Thomas* arrived.

The railway journey between Bristol and Cardiff had been

shortened to thirty-eight miles, but there were no heavy freight facilities.

In the meantime, the tunnel was progressing then, when it opened, the ferry trade was killed. Ships were sold and piers allowed to rot. But with the growth of car traffic after the war they ferry started again with diesel-powered ships. Repairs were made, a café was opened on the east side and once again, Old Passage at Aust throbbed with activity until its final death knell.

The first Severn Bridge was opened in 1966, followed thirty years later by the second crossing.

Now all traces of this ancient river crossing have gone except for some rotting timbers and the red and grey cliffs. But this tiny portion of England left an indelible mark on our history.

Filton

Filton and Horfield have always been like cheese and onion with little Ham tucked in as the extra filling. They were only one small part of the Hundred of Berkeley and made two simple parishes.

Oddly enough, Filton had only a few early names which were Fylton, Phylton and also Feltham. The name of Hay comes from Haia or La Haye while Horfleld's name meant open countryside from the words horu and feld.

Neither of them had brilliant soil; it was always poor with stiff clay and very hard to work, virtually impossible with early, primitive tools. This is why for many, long centuries it was wild land, right until King Henry III, who authorised disafforestation in 1228. Large areas of woodland did still remain until 1813, which is difficult to visualise today with its heavily built-up residential streets.

It was always well and truly a Berkeley region but before this family, one famous resident was Tighere, who in 770 was consecrated the Bishop of Worcester in 777. This man's name though can be spelled in a variety of ways probably because of the clerks of the day.

Lady Goda, who was the sister of Edward the Confessor, is known to have held lands at Filton before the Domesday Book. Then the Earldom of Berkeley was granted to Robert Fitzharding as a reward for his services during the dreadful civil war between King Stephen and his cousin the empress Matilda, sometimes called Maud. For this friendship, Henry Plantagenet, later King Henry II, confirmed this grant.

It is not at all clear on whose side Fitzharding gave his favours but at a time which was shocking for the peasants, nobles themselves were very quick to change sides to suit themselves. Total loyalty was inclined to be lacking as each man preferred to look after his own.

Henry II was a pragmatic and highly active man. He also had enormous charisma with men – as well as with the ladies except his wife – and he wanted to be king very much. He was also determined to wear the crown so he too was not above a fair amount of bribery to keep the fighting men very much under his royal thumb.

Long before all this, the Romans were around as they were just about everywhere. Some traces of an early settlement dating back to 340AD have been found but the greatest pointer to their occupation was made in 1880.

On an April day, a young artisan was out gathering primroses, obviously for his sweetheart. On the bank of a brook at Filton he must have become bored then he saw a piece of potsherd. In typical young male fashion it promptly turned into an interesting target. He hurled a stone at it and his aim was very accurate. It was spot on then the young man had the shock of his life. The pot shattered completely and out poured a huge quantity of Roman coins.

Some unconfirmed reports say there were as many as 3,000 pieces many of which had been minted during the reign of

Constantine the Great. The amazed young man grabbed as many as he could carry then did a rapid runner with his unexpected treasure, primrose-collecting very much forgotten.

What exactly happened to all these coins is most unclear in the old records. Some found homes in museums but it is highly likely the bulk vanished into lofts and attics and gradually became forgotten.

Later on though it is recorded that a Mr Jones of BAC also found some coins which appear to have been discovered by his late uncle near to the bottom of Filton Hill but where have all these gone?

Domesday tells us there were only eight householders in Filton in the eleventh century and it is likely that half of these probably lived at Horfield. It is known that the family de Filton lived in the parish and were the lords of the manor. Doubtless they were also connected with the Berkeley family.

Elias de Filton held the land in 1156 and one member of this family was chosen as a knight in 1247/8 to be a member of a jury for the Hundred of Berkeley. This confirms they were an upper-class family and also had to have owned a certain amount of land to make the knight's fee.

We also know that another de Filton was taxed in 1346 the sum of five marks for a war horse which was always a very expensive animal. During this period, the name of Filton was spelled in the variety of ways until it finally settled at that which we know today. One little part was, in these early days, called Filton le Haye and this name held even as late as 1870.

Hayes farm used to run westwards to today's A38 road. It was opposite the current Gipsy Patch Lane whose earlier name was simply The Gipsyies Patch. All this was wiped out when the runway was extended for the Brabazon.

Early Filton had many streams known as Batches so it must have been a pretty wet place. We do know that in 1770 new stocks were erected for petty crimes at the high cost of £3.15.11 in old money and this came from the Poor Rates.

Initially policing was conducted from the police station at Hambrook and Westbury then a station was built at Horfield which answered for Filton. It is thought possible a constable was finally stationed at Filton by 1895 but he would be on Horfield's strength.

Old deeds show that Elizabeth Pope had three farms, one of which was at the place known as Conygre. As far back as 1703 Jacob Millett is mentioned as owning the messuage of Cunigre which was a farm of ninety-six acres. Following this there were various tenancies down the decades until Conygre House became the country seat of Isaac Niblett.

He became one of the great farmers of Filton and also owned the White Lion in 1823. He was also very well-known in the coaching world.

The New House, later Filton House, was built around 1773 and owned by the Latcham family. This too was an excellent farm. Down the years many families lived there until it became the property of Samuel Shields who sold out, just prior to World War I, to the British and Colonial Aeroplane Company.

There were three main families at Filton, the Wades, the Milletts and the Gayners. The Wades have always been considered the senior family with the longest connection to Filton. A very early Wade was a church warden in 1498 at a time when the parish was known as Philton. It is this family who produced Nathaniel Wade who was so highly involved with the Duke of Monmouth in the seventeenth century.

At that period Jacob Millett, a felt-maker and from Frampton Cotterell, obtained a lease on Conygre House and its lands for twenty-one years. It is thought he finished felt-making and took up farming instead. Certainly six generations of his family had connections with the property.

The Gayners too are considered to have farmed in the area for as many generations though this would have to take into account people's shorter life spans. An interesting snippet tells us that between 1758-69, twenty people only lived at Filton who were married at the parish church. Of these thirteen were unable to sign the register because they were illiterate!

In today's heavily built-up Filton with its world-famous industry, it is hard to imagine that, not all those many decades ago, Filton had huge, lumbering farm wagons moving along very rough tracks and people were born, lived and died without even setting foot in Bristol.

We call it progress, don't we?

Forest of Dean

This lovely part of the country with its hardwood trees, gives us a very good idea what the whole of England looked like a few thousand years ago. Although we do have forests elsewhere, the Forest of Dean is probably the best known and loved. It lies between the Severn and Wye rivers and covers 204 square miles or 528 sq kms. It has high sandstone ridges and gentle valleys and became an official National Park in 1939. Some of the sandstone lies over carboniferous limestone and this latter was popular in the Middle Ages as a substitute for marble.

Its name still arouses some controversy with the historians. One school of thought holds that this originates from Mitcheldean also called Dean Magna in the Domesday Book. This is in a valley though the word Dean or Dene is Saxon and means a dale or den. The next school insists it come from a statement made by one Giraldus and the name comes from the Danes. Many of them did shelter in this area with its shades and thickets because here they felt safe from people whose homes they devastated on a regular basis. The third school states the name arises from Arden which, less a syllable, makes Dean and comes from the Old British.

We do know that prior to 1066 it was in the Hundred of William, son of Norman and there were three thanes with their homes there called Godric, Alric and Ernwy. The Domesday Book records there were thirty-eight smallholders but does not mention servi or slaves which is rather unusual. It does agree that King Edward assigned the whole area as being one exempt from any tax in return for the forest being 'guarded'.

We also know that in 1069 William I was enjoying himself out hunting in the Forest when news reached him the Danes had invaded Yorkshire. He was enraged and vowed that 'not one Northumbrian would escape his revenge'. They did not.

It is reasonable to deduce that on one of his visits, the miners applied for and were granted their unique customs and franchises which would only have been a continuation of those given by King Edward. These canny miners were just covering their backs with the new Norman ruler.

For once the Romans were well and truly beaten to it by the Celts who were the very early inhabitants of this land. The Celts were one of the first also to exploit the abundant natural resources of iron and coal although there was only a little of the latter in Roman times. Iron was far more important for people who fought with metal. It is from this race we have the word Scowles as it is Old British and means caves and also the old iron workings.

Many Roman remains have been found ranging from cinders, coins, brass images, tesserae and bricks as well as a Roman pavement. There were also Roman roads and some may even be recognised today with their higher elevation of drainage which is a typical Roman feature.

It was in the thirteenth century that men were allowed to mine on their own accord. This right was given to them by Edward I in 1300 as his gift for the men's help in the siege of Berwick on Tweed. These rights and customs are set out clearly in the Book of Dennis. The men guarded these precious rights fiercely and still do today. They consider themselves the aristocrats of the Forest and are just a little inclined to pity those who lack Forest status.

There was always the danger of trouble from the Welsh so the castle of St Briavels, sometimes called Brulails in the old records, was erected by Milo Fitz-Walter with the sole object of enforcing royal authority in the area. Not long after this another old record confirms that Gloucester was supplied with iron and venison by the noble and Royal Forest of Dean.

King Stephen took a great interest in the Forest as also did King John but with the latter it was always the chase. Nearly all of the kings turned up, at some time or the other during their reigns, simply for the hunting available.

The old copy extant of the *Miners' Laws and Privileges* was held to be a kind of Magna Carta of the miners and colliers. It was printed in 1687 by William Cooper at The Pelican in Little Britain. This came from an earlier manuscript written on a parchment roll held by Richard Morse in 1673. These precious rights were those granted 'time out of mind'.

A brother of Rogerus, Earl of Hereford, was killed with an arrow out hunting and this death eventually led to the erection of an Abbey about 1140 in Stephen's reign. The Bishop of Hereford was heavily involved and it was called the Abbey of St Mary of Dene or simply Dene Abbey. It was devoted to the monks of the Cistercian Order.

The monks' dress was a white cassock with a narrow scapulary and it is thought, from this, comes the name of St Whites in Little Dean as well as Whitecross.

Henry VIII suppressed all of the country's abbeys and it was granted to Sir William Kinston, the Constable of the Tower of London.

Coleford is considered the 'capital' and is the district seat while Cinderford and Mitcheldean, all former mining centres, are known as parishes or towns of the Forest. They are places where people live, where tourists throng and in their surrounds sheep and cattle graze freely.

The Speech House is very near to Coleford and is a court of the wood. Some people refer to this as the King's Walk, so called after Charles II. There is also York Walk or Lodge plus other walks with their lodges. The former is so called as its intended use was for the ancient Court of 'the Speech' as is mentioned in the *Laws and Franchises of the Mine*. Always held before the Verderers, the 'law' of the area.

In the Speech house there are definite formalities because a mine court has always been a serious affair with a constable, a clerk, the gaveller and a miners' jury. This could comprise twelve, twenty-four or forty-eight men in cases relating to the mines. Three 'hands' or three witnesses were necessary for evidence and the oath was taken with a stick of holly in the hand. Miners of Mitcheldean, Little Deane and Ruer Deane were and are called 'beneath the wood'.

The rules to be a Forest miner are very clear indeed. Any man who wishes to be called a free miner must have been born within the Hundred of St Briavel which was a very old land measurement and still recognised today. The man must have worked for one year and one day in the mines. This gives him the right to be called a Free Miner and carries with it the boon to open new seams.

Strictly speaking, the word miner was used to denote one who dug for iron ore. Collier meant a man who worked for coal but this has all become a little loose and interchangeable though little iron ore working is now done.

It is the Gaveller, on behalf of the crown, who regulates the award of the gales and this is the name given to the place where coal is worked. He also collects dues from the free miners. Many of the older men can be recognised as retired miners because they carry the permanent blue scars on their skins and bodies.

Today some of these rights now extend to quarrying for stone but this is only done on a fairly small scale.

The old colliers and miners were a savagely independent breed. Many lived in disused mine caves or primitive huts which they built in clearings. Around them was all the timber and fuel which they needed and they were near to their place of labour. These were often drift mines though there was a commercial colliery but this closed in 1965.

Above ground there is another type of open cast mining which is done by Outsiders who have always caused enormous controversy and more than a few rough fights.

Great danger arose to the Royal Forest from two directions. One came from the charcoal burners but the other was much more serious as it involved the Royal Navy. With the burners, wood was consumed in vast quantities and it was all done in a most irresponsible manner. In 1640, the crown leased the Forest and its contents to Sir John Winter. He was utterly ruthless and started to decimate the Forest with no thought for the future. He felled trees drastically, never once stopping to think how long it takes a tree to grow. He chopped and felled to such an extent that Parliament had to step in. There were only 200 trees left.

In 1688, The Dean Forest Reafforestation Act was passed by some wise men and so started the controlled administration of the Forest but it was only just in the nick of time. Today's Forest goes back to this excellent Act because steps were taken to preserve it. Enclosures were set up, each of about 11,000 acres and here trees were planted. They were divided into areas or walks all of which had a guardian keeper.

The old Verderer's Court was revived, which had power over life and limb, and it became responsible for settling Forestry disputes. In the seventeenth and eighteenth centuries, holly trees were thought to have been planted. At the same time, iron mining was discouraged because of its need for charcoal, which consumed too much timber.

There was serious trouble in 1735 when the keepers reported squatters were felling trees and burning the undergrowth. The great problem was these squatters were free miners with rights established long ago by a monarch. They had no intention of giving up these rights either.

The Verderers' Court had to solve this dispute without ruffling the feathers of men who had no hesitation in fighting to guard their rights. As most of the free miners were very careful to marry only within their tight-knit community, it was like dealing with awkward and belligerent foreigners. Today there are still a number of free miners who are every bit as jealous of their rights as their forebears.

Today the Forest is administered most carefully with huge emphasis upon the ecology and mixed woodland's management. There is abundant wild flora and fauna, wonderful to observe away from the hazards of chemicals. Nature as it was intended to be from the start of time without man's obnoxious interference.

On the 18th February 1662 there was a dreadful storm in the night, of which Samuel Pepys wrote saying he had received letters from the Forest, which said about 1,000 oaks and as many beeches were blown down. All roads were impassable and in some great 'orchards' it was possible to go from one end to the other, without touching the ground.

The Rev John Wesley established a connection with the people of the Forest and visited Coleford in 1757 and again in 1763, which facts are recorded in his journal. No great effort was made though to impart religious instructions to the Foresters until 1803.

In this year, the Rev Proctor became the vicar of Newlands and he was wise. He moved slowly and only took an afternoon duty at Coleford Chapel when invited. The miners turned up from sheer curiosity but they must have been impressed because others followed this lead. Before long this preacher had started a course of lectures and congregations increased enormously. It was this that then led to the construction of a proper lecture room and, gradually, schools, so the Foresters were able to elevate themselves.

The Forest has always had a rare inhabitant, which nearly spelled its doom. The oak of Dean has always been considered the best tree in the world. It has to grow upon poor soil and so developed a short trunk with an enormous spreading habit. As it grew very slowly, its timber became exceedingly strong and it was this particular oak tree which the shipbuilders demanded for England's wooden walls at sea. It was pure luck the advent of steel ships halted this destruction.

In 1812 an idea was mooted to dig a tunnel under the Severn so men started work. They were defeated by an incredible phenomenon. They had to abandon the whole idea because of the water which came into their tunnel – from below! Obviously from some powerful underground stream.

Symonds Yat is a beauty spot which cries out to be visited as well as the rivers. Salmon have always been fished from the Severn by men called putchers who use lave nets. Awre is a fairly popular place although the fishing is strictly controlled.

Many Foresters have the right to keep sheep which are allowed to roam. This causes huge problems when a disease like foot and mouth breaks out.

There are hikers' trails throughout the Forest and one is guarded by a sculpture called the Giant Chair. This is on the Sculptors' trail. It is possible to hire cycles to explore. For steam buffs there is a narrow gauge railway at Parrygrove while at Lydney Junction, there is also a standard gauge steam railway. Cinderford has the excellent Dean Heritage Centre which is filled with information enough to satisfy the most curious.

It is a splendid treat to visit the Royal Forest of Dean and to 'go back in time'.

Hawkesbury

This is a bit like a dual village. Hawkesbury and the Upton part on the higher ground.

It had eighteen names of old, two of which are Hovochesberie and Hawkesbyr. It is thought most of the old names come from Hafoc's fortified palace but, frustratingly, there is no clue about Hafoc himself. He must have been a freeman of some standing to require fortifications in the first place.

The Upton bit is situated on reasonably high ground which makes the last point of the Cotswolds before it slides down to a lower elevation. Even though not as high as other parts of the county, there are some superb views.

The best views of all though are from the top of the monument which the Beauforts erected in memory of Lord Robert Edward Henry Somerset, sometimes known as Rupert Somerset.

He fought with valour and distinction at Waterloo. There are 144 steps to the top of his monument. From this high point it is possible to see well into the Malverns in one direction. To the west is the River Severn, the Forest of Dean and the Welsh mountains. To the south west there is the Bristol Channel and the island of Flat Holm near Weston Super Mare. To the east is Salisbury Plain. It all makes remarkable viewing, with the right weather conditions, but, to climb to the top, very athletic knees are required.

Tradition has it that Oswald, King of Mercia, founded a college of secular canons at Hawkesbury though it is not thought this was at the Upton site. This was in 984 and was, in due course, replaced with a Benedictine community.

It is positive though the church has Saxon workmanship. Only they could have built the bases of the shafts of the inner doorway. It is possible these were laid by tenth-century monks. It is upon these basic but splendid foundations that the Normans let their builders take over.

It is well-known that in the old days women liked to wear pattens on their feet to avoid the thick mud. There was a firm order that women left both their dogs and their pattens at home. They most certainly could not enter the church wearing pattens.

This little place has some famous names associated with it. One of the first, after King Oswald, was St Wulfstan who was there between 1033 and 1038. Later this great man became the Bishop of Worcester. Despite the Conquest he still, somehow, retained his office until after the death of William I. St Wulfstan died in 1095 and was buried at Worcester Cathedral.

In the thirteenth century Hawkesbury had its own fulling mill, property of the lord of the manor. Whether the tenants were enthusiastic we don't know. Probably not. If they took their wares elsewhere, the lord of the manor promptly fined them. These mills were owned by lords of the manor and their demanded use gave the lords quite a nice revenue.

From the top of the hill, without undue climbing, it is possible to see the many rhines from the river's estuary. In other parts of the country they will be called ditches or dykes.

Over 2,000 years ago the land below Hawkesbury Upton would have been wet, muddy, darkly forested and highly dangerous. A place a wise traveller avoided.

For many centuries the whole region was owned by the Abbey of Pershore. This abbey also had the grant of the markets, fairs and free warrens. It also had a court leet. A court of record held periodically in the Hundred before the lord or his steward. It held jurisdiction over all petty offences as well as the area civil affairs.

An action in Quo Warranto was brought against the Abbey in which they had to prove they had the right to all which they claimed. Being an abbey they soon did this.

At the dissolution of the monasteries, the manor was granted to John Butler and, through marriages, passed into the hands of the Jenkinson family. We now come to two stories about this family, one remarkable and the other incredibly sad.

The most famous of the Jenkinsons was the second Earl Sir Robert. He was only five weeks old when his mother brought him to Hawkesbury from London. The mother herself was a mere nineteen years so must have had a worrying journey when travel was difficult and dangerous. She must have been very stressed because she never saw her own home again.

⋙∞⋘

Little Robert grew and entered Parliament. He then had the fortune or misfortune to be there when a madman assassinated the Prime Minister, Mr Spencer Percival. Sir Robert became the Prime Minister in his stead at the worrying time of Waterloo. Lord Liverpool of Hawkesbury was quite a remarkable man at a difficult time of our history.

The other is poignant and tragic in its telling. A daughter of the Jenkinsons fell in love with a neighbour's son, Mr Paston. The Jenkinsons were ardent Protestants. The Pastons were dedicated Catholics.

The young couple did not care in the least about this religious difference. Both sets of parents did though. A harsh feud developed, as all four parents were violently opposed to any match.

The end was that young Paston was barred from the Jenkinson home. The day came when the lovers were ordered to say 'goodbye'. It was Romeo and Juliet again.

With breaking hearts they parted. Miss Jenkinson leant out of the oriel window waving to her lover, vowing her undying love, crying to him. She overbalanced and fell to her death.

Not long afterwards, the family moved from the house. Later in the twenty-eighth century, the Sixth Baronet loaned the house to his cousin Charles. He was set to bring his new, young wife there after the birth of their son.

Once again tragedy struck. The young wife died on the journey and it was her body which was brought to the manor to be buried in the local church.

After that, understandably, the old Jenkinson house lost all popularity. It was abandoned and allowed to fall into ruins.

It is almost macabre that a house, in such a place and with beautiful views, could be associated with young death.

Are there ghosts there? Who knows? Certainly the lost young hearts must hover in the air around which such great hopes had been built so long ago.

Iron Acton

Iron Acton's early history is a little bit confusing compared to many other villages. To start with, the Iron portion was absent. The Acton word came from Actune or Ass et Greq, Ass. It was also known, centuries ago, as Acton Ilger, Ilger or even under the Old German Hildegar.

This latter name is particularly interesting. After the Romans had pulled out, the British and Romano-British had to learn how to fight again. In a panic, many of them hired mercenaries – quite a number of which came from the land we know of today as Germany. So does the name Hildegar indicate at least one German mercenary in this region? Quite unproven but thought-provoking.

The word Iron was only added later to distinguish the village from Acton Turville and means literally iron coming from Iren. This tells us there had to be iron workings and evidence was found centuries later because of the huge amount of cinders lying around.

The original name is thought to mean farmstead near an oak tree or oak trees in general. As iron needs fire to make the ore malleable, this needed timber. The halting of all the iron works tells us that they simply ran out of suitable trees for these fires.

It was in the Bagstone Hundred and the Bishop of Lo held the area. Domesday tells us that it held four villages, five smallholders, one male and two female slaves. This latter point makes an unusual imbalance even though slaves could be bred very much as cattle are today. How Christian was this bishop then?

Early records murmur about a coal pit but in those days of non-record-keeping it is difficult, if not impossible, to work out where this stood. Later Coal Board maps do not help much either.

As the whole region held coal, it can only be presumed that in this village there may have been shallow workings, possibly only a narrow seam.

The River Frome, which rises at Dodington, receives the Ladden Brook at this village before it runs on into Bristol to form part of the port.

Before Domesay we do know there were two distinct estates with three villains, three bordars and just two slaves but there was also a mill.

John de Acton, who was most likely descended from the Earls of Hereford, took the village's name as his own which was perfectly normal then. His grandson also had a court leet and, remarkably, a fallows and tumbrel. But how much hanging took place is not known.

In those days when documents were often lost by fire or sheer carelessness, the Crown would make estate and manor owners prove they had the right of ownership. It was a crafty way by the Crown to extort money.

If they failed to prove the estate was theirs to the Crown's satisfaction, the Crown just grabbed it and that was that. Or, more practically, the Crown would issue a heavy fine to the owners.

The last de Acton was Sir John who died in 1344. The manor then passed to his cousin Maud, the widow of Sir Nicholas Poyntz. The Poyntz males seemed to be men with a sharp eye at all times for personal and family advantages. One of them grabbed the stonework from Kingswood Arch near Wotton when it was going to be demolished. Another made the mistake of trying to cross swords figuratively with a titled lady at Yate. He came off very much the worse when she not only trounced him but hauled him before the notorious Star Chamber.

That cooled the Poyntz ideas for a while, then they mingled with royalty. One Poyntz entertained Henry VII in his manor house. Elizabeth I was also received at a refurbished manor house. All this mixing with royalty meant money because it was not just the monarch who had to be entertained, fed and lodged, but also the vast retinue.

The Poyntz family, descended from Normans who came over with William I, were proud of their breeding and position but entertaining royalty must have cast a considerable strain upon their purse strings.

One of them was a scholar. Sir Robert Poyntz, Knight of the Bath at the coronation of Charles I, also wrote a treatise in Vindication of his monarch. He died in 1265 – five years before the Puritan Commonwealth collapsed and the monarchy was restored to Charles II.

The little village had another visitor of great note who stayed at the manor but one who precipitated almighty panic among the ladies. It was Sir Walter Raleigh. The story goes that one day, while strolling around the garden, he lit his pipe without thinking.

All the ladies were appalled and fled in utter horror at this man who had set himself on fire. What Sir Walter must have thought is not recorded. He had acquired his tobacco in lands where it was usual to smoke.

The last Poyntz died in 1680 and was buried in the local church. The Poyntzs died out and the manor, after being in one family for 600 years, was brought by William Player, after which Sir Samuel Astry owned it.

It is interesting to note that during the reign of Henry VIII a messuage in Iron Acton belonged to the Magdalen Hospital in Bristol but it has to be deduced this was some kind of gift, probably to help the poor and sick.

Nothing of great note or fame occurred in Iron Acton. Perhaps just because it was so tranquil it attracted people. It has its little monuments and always to the Poyntz family. There is an old cross in the churchyard and it was Robert Poyntz who rebuilt the church.

Who had the idea of a maypole on the village green is not recorded. Certainly a maypole is more pagan than Christian but the early churches had long ago learned to live with the people's favourites. A maypole stands there to this day and it is not incongruous even in the twenty-first century. It fits in very well with the village's tranquillity.

Today the by-pass has removed all traffic and the main street, loaded with ancient cottages, can give us a very good idea of what a genuine English village was like for centuries.

Kingswood

They were called the savages of Kingswood and feared by all, especially the people of Bristol and Bath.

They were considered lower than navvies, a breed with whom decent people never associated. They caused terror because of a discipline more formal than the military. So who were these barbarians, and why did they have this name?

The miners of Kingswood, like all of their breed, had a unique camaraderie. Since two men first went underground to dig for coal, they evolved a natural brotherhood of 'all for one and one for all'. It was a creed which put Freemasonry into a kindergarten class.

Perhaps, too, they were savages with good reason. They often lived far worse than animals, through no fault of their own. Their homes were crude sod and turf shacks with no facilities. Their children were uneducated and starvation was never far away.

Their wages, although a little above that of agricultural workers, worked out less because colliers had no farm perks. Also, their lives were in constant danger due to the nature of their work. Death always sat on their shoulders.

In 1708 there was a terrible harvest and bread prices went beyond the colliers' pockets. The weather was bitterly cold up to the middle of April.

On 21st May, 400 colliers marched on Bristol to demand food.

Even Bristol's own poor flocked to support them as home-grown wheat was exported despite England's own starving people.

Bristol magistrates told the colliers that wheat would be available the next day at 6s 8d (33p) per bushel (8 gallons or 36.4 litres). Satisfied, the colliers began to return home to Kingswood but on hearing that some of their more vocal members had been arrested, they about-turned and marched back to challenge Bristol. Very quickly, those arrested were allowed to 'escape'.

In 1726 there was more trouble, with riots over the charges at turnpikes. The militia was called out, so the colliers refused to let any coal enter Bristol. Bristol ceded, and coal became exempt from turnpike tolls although the price rose from 1s (5p) to 2s 3d (11p) for a horse-load in consequence.

At about this time, in 1730, the foundations of Methodism were laid by George Whitfield and John Wesley. They were acutely aware of the Kingswood colliers' fierce reputation. The year before, Whitfield had started open-air meetings before sixty colliers who were then arrested after a street riot. A further meeting drew a crowd of 20,000.

John Wesley was not keen to start with, but then he, too, became converted to field preaching and for the next fifty-two years was an itinerant preacher to the common folk. There was no overnight conversion of the colliers. People still retreated behind bolted doors and shuttered windows when the colliers were out in force. In 1743 a mob of colliers even attacked the homes of known Methodists and destroyed all their furniture. Ten years later there were more riots when, once again, the price of bread rose too high for the colliers' families.

Bristol's mayor pacified the men but some colliers acted on their own initiative and started unloading grain from ships at Bristol Docks. Constables with drawn swords took many prisoners and the main body of colliers began to smash windows and throw stones. Three days later, more men marched into the city and the Scots Greys arrived. Two thousand colliers then attacked at a cost of four lives. Many men were wounded before everything eventually quietened and bread and grain became available again.

The inhabitants of Bristol were now in an uproar at these goings-on in their city by the savages from Kingswood.

It was not until 1775 that colliers were at liberty to leave a mine where they were employed until the end of a contract, usually five years. They were even transferred with the lease to any new owner. Under the Habeas Corpus Act colliers, like sailors, were exempt from any of its provisions and were virtual slaves.

Wesley's work, though, had a great impact upon the colliers even if it had a slow start. Religious fervour began to sweep the men's ranks. Organised night-watch services became a great feature of Methodism, antagonising the Anglican Church. Gradually, the colliers realised that someone was, at last, on their side.

In 1756 the first friendly society was formed for colliers and the inaugural meeting was held at The White Hart at Hanham, with further meetings held monthly on Saturday evenings. Fines of 2d were imposed for smoking or drinking at these times. Contributions were fixed at 10d (4p) per month. There was a benefit of 7s (35p) per week, but injuries due to fighting were excluded. The society gave a £5 death benefit, of which £2 was for the man's funeral and £3 for his widow.

There was a special day set aside for a feast on St John's Day, 24th June. This would become the highlight of the collier's year. With the life of hard toil, risk to health and death always hovering, any relief became welcome.

Men who lived like this could not be expected to have a pacific nature – they could even be called remarkably restrained when their lives were compared to the citizens of Bristol who were kept warm and cosy through their efforts.

In 1833 the societies for the mutual relief of colliers became stressed. There was a terrible outbreak of cholera which depleted their funds. An appeal was made for the distressed poor of Kingswood, so an attempt was made to instil hygiene into these people's lives. This proved impossible and filth and blocked drains abounded.

Slowly, though, public conscience became aroused by the local religious organisations. George Pocock, the grandfather of the famous W G Grace, and father of an Anglican clergyman, turned to Methodism. It was he who founded the Tent Methodists for Sunday services to which people flocked. But he, too, was always short of cash. His heart was in the right place, though, and this the colliers realised.

Slowly the savages became 'tamed' as their conditions improved. They also acquired the same freedom as other men to move jobs.

In the twentieth century, all the pits closed and they are long gone from the landscape. But surely we should understand what these colliers suffered and why they were not really savages?

Royal Forest Of Kingswood

Kingswood, Bristol is not really a very accurate name because it really described a fairly large forest which belonged exclusively to the king.

Although gloomy under certain weather conditions, it was never permanently dark like today's forests of softwood pine trees.

A millennium ago, the trees were deciduous and of hardwood, comprising oaks, beeches, birches, ash and chestnut. They were greatly prized for their hardness in weapon-making and, centuries later, it was trees of this calibre which were taken for shipbuilding to make the 'wooden walls' of England.

Today's Yate is down in Domesday Book as Giete and it is thought this was meant to indicate it was indeed one of the gates to the King's Wood.

Some portions of this wood had clearings in which low-growing shrubs, bushes and gorse thrived, and the whole region was a haven for wildlife much of it, fortunately, extinct today. The predatory animals then were the wolf, bear and boar, and the more gentle deer.

Unless starving, a pack of wolves would not often attack a healthy, armed male although the young and old might be taken if the pack were desperate from starvation. Only the alpha male could decide this, because a wolf pack was highly disciplined.

Bears were unpredictable and dangerous, perfectly capable of overtaking a running man. It only needed one blow from a heavily-clawed paw to bring a man down and break his neck.

Boars too were not to be trifled with, especially when a sow had young. Boar and deer were hunted for meat, although venison was only ever the king's meat. It was considered far too rich and good for serfs, and was reserved exclusively for the king and his nobles.

All the kings were jealous of their deer and severe laws were in force to protect them from serfs. Any poacher caught with deer meat was almost certain to be executed. Most serfs' hounds had certain claws removed to eliminate their ability to chase after deer.

In those days the chasm between the 'haves' and the 'have nots' was so enormous that today's 'have nots' would have been regarded as living in luxury. Desperate men with families to feed would chance poaching deer. One such trespasser was Matthew de Button who was caught red-handed. He was tried and, because it was not his first offence, he was executed.

Sometimes the lower classes were able to acquire certain rights. One was furcas or furchis cutting, in which they were allowed to take a certain amount of wood from the forest edges for their fires or fences.

Another perquisite given to them at times was the right, in the autumn, to run their pigs at the forest edge so they might fatten up on fallen acorns.

The kings were often short of money so, now and again, they

would sell off small portions of their forests for hard coin to people who wanted the trees or land to start a smallholding.

It is from these small, early sections of land that little villages sprang up. Although King's Wood was small compared to the great New Forest or that at Rockingham, it was popular with the kings and their nobles.

Many travelled there to hunt and enjoy the mounted chase, residing at the Royal Saxon palace at Pucklechurch, which has long since vanished.

It was not many years after this that kings and nobles began to take a serious interest in conservation. They were probably the first 'green' party in existence, but it was from no form of altruism. It was to protect their noble rights or the chase and the kill.

Men were engaged to look after the trees and animals. Gradually, down the decades, the kings continued to sell off portions of the King's Wood because when ship-building was a great industry, the kings made great sums from these sales.

After that came the discovery of coal so, again, land was sold off this time for mining rights. This, in turn, meant miners had to have homes nearby so more land went for cottages. The advent of coal-mining was probably the death knell of the great King's Wood.

Villages began to proliferate and their modern names tell us the extent of the King's Wood. Leigh means a forest clearing, as at Westerleigh. Wick meant an outlying farm, while Ham speaks of pastureland or water meadows, as in today's Hanham.

The same kind of detective work can suggest a person's ancestor's work; Carpenter, Turner, Smith and so on. They all go back down the centuries to when land belonged solely to a king, which helps us see a picture of what life was like a millennium ago.

Little Sodbury

The Roman fort at Little Sodbury was so well sited that, on a clear day, fourteen villages could be seen with the naked eye. At one time, most of the country was still heavily forested, but pluming smoke gave away small, inhabited areas.

This camp is on the edge of the Cotswolds and follows the usual Roman pattern, a parallelogram. It covered about twelve acres.

All Roman forts and even overnight camps were constructed exactly the same all over the vast empire. This was sound policy, because it meant new men joining knew exactly where everything should be. Weapons were always – here, latrines – there.

The west side of the camp only had a slight bank for defence because, at its rear, was a very steep hill. Even the bloody-minded Britons were incapable of climbing this, then fighting.

It is thought the fort was large enough to hold three cohorts of Romans and six of their allied soldiers, with an appropriate number of cavalry. This would total 4,500 men.

These would be men from the XXth Legion, based at Glevum, today's Gloucester. Like all Roman soldiers, they were tough, highly-disciplined warriors. On the march or stamping into battle, they made an awesome military spectacle. They marched in step, often sang bawdy songs and answered the officers' whistles with every boot stamped in unison. Words of command were not given.

They were inclined to stink but this was not the fetid smell of filth. It was a combination of healthy sweat from heavily armed men capable of marching thirty miles every day, and their dress was leather, which had to be constantly oiled for preservation, so this too carried an unusual bouquet.

All of this was the exact opposite of the native Britons who, in this region, were of the Dubonii tribe. To the Britons, fighting was an honourable occupation, entertainment, even a hobby.

They were perfectly happy to submit a single champion to fight the Romans' champion for sheer fun.

The Romans scorned such ill-bred behaviour. It was a complete culture clash and the finale was inevitable. What Rome never imagined, though, was that these difficult Druid-worshippers would eventually require the vast number of 50,000 hardened troops to subdue them.

In the middle of the first century, the governor of Britain was Publius Ostorius Scapula and he fumed all the time. His own health was precarious. He was totally unenthusiastic about the wet, misty island. He considered the Britons an ungrateful lot and had to juggle his men of the XXth Legion based at Glevum to subdue them.

Like all Romans, Scapula believed in steady government, a positive hierarchy and old-fashioned bureaucracy. The Dubonii were unimpressed. It was their land. They had not asked the Romans to invade.

Scapula was nobody's fool though. He quickly realised the British warriors, female as well as male, were incredibly brave and often egged on by the hated Druids. They were pitiful against the hard might of a Legion, but they excelled at Guerrilla tactics and were extremely dangerous terrorists.

Forage parties constantly had to be sent out to take from the land, yet no soldier dared relax his guard. At any time, a band of hard-fighting Britons could swoop from the trees and Roman bodies were the result.

To start with, an edict went out that no Britons could hold weapons. They could only keep second-rate spears for hunting. But they simply hooted at this and placed their battle weapons in secret hideouts. No Romans searching their huts ever found any.

Scapula was powerless to do anything. He fumed and boiled and issued another edict. He ordered that the Silures tribe over the River Severn was to be decimated. All males over twelve would be slaughtered and the females taken as slaves. It was ethnic cleansing of the most vicious sort.

It fused the Britons into a cohesive mass. Old tribal enmities were forgotten once Scapula's order became known. Although Rome eventually conquered, it might have been easier with a political solution.

It is unclear whether Scapula died here or on a journey back to Rome but he was well-known for his short fuse.

Go and visit the site of the fort. You can park on the lane then climb the hill. Do not take the drive on one side which leads to the Little Sodbury Manor, as this is private. At the top, with the aid of a map from the Bristol and Glos Archaeological Records, it is fairly easy to work out the precise site.

At the same time, admire the stunning view and think perhaps of all the hassle Scapula had when governor at this fort.

Marshfield

Marshfield was in the Hundred of Edderstone and in Domesday was marked down as Terra Regis. In other words, it belonged to the royals and one of high rank, too.

In the old days it had thirteen names, all with slightly different spellings and far too many to enumerate, but two are Meresfelde and Maresfeld.

From the sound of the current name one immediately associates the village with marshy land. Nothing could be farther from the truth. The land is high up, overlooking the surrounding countryside.

The Old English says that Meresfelde meant, quite simply, open land by a pool or alternatively a tract of open land by a boundary. This latter is a more accurate translation because there are three boundaries nearby – Gloucestershire, Wiltshire and Somerset – which makes it unique.

It is thought the area had been lived in for at least three

millennia, though the discovery of Bronze Age artefacts have been thin on the ground.

What did come to light in 1968 was something that had the historians breaking into a gallop to get there. A gas pipe trench was being dug at nearby West Littleton Down when two skeletons were unearthed. The bones were dated and found to be from about 970BC. They were of two young males and their manner of death was obvious. Fragments of the spearheads which had killed them were still embedded in their bones.

The nearby places of Tormarton, Didmarton and Rodmarton come under Marshfield. Some hold that these three names derive from Mars, the God of War. The jury, though, is still out on this one.

Marshfield itself stands roughly in the centre of the inhabited area with a rather long main street. The major turnpike road from London arrived here because Marshfield was the final stopping place for coaches before it dropped down into Bath. This made Marshfield very important indeed.

All around the region is evidence of tumuli or barrows, the largest of which was called Oswald's Tump. The story goes that Oswald and Penda, of Mercia, had a huge battle here. At this time the Mercians and the Northumbrians were constantly at each other's throats, striving for dominance. On this occasion it was the turn of the Mercians and some people suggest Marshfield's name derives from Mercia. This, though, is pretty threadbare and quite unproven.

The victory was supposed to be a great event for the Mercians and the Northumbrians' king was killed very near to Marshfield. Tradition had it that Oswald's body was exposed by the Mercians on a crude cross. Oswiu, sometimes known as Oswy, was brother to the hapless Oswald. He must have seethed with rage at these upstart Mercians. He met them in battle and it was Northumbria's turn to win.

Penda died on the banks of the stream called Winwaed at a place called Loidis, today's Leeds. His body was never recovered.

The victor always demanded tribute over the loser. So Mercia came under Northumbria's thumb until a suitably strong king like Wulfhere arose.

They had to pay tribute in Mercia just as the Northumbrians had been forced to pay tribute to the Mercians, the people who lived in South Gloucestershire. It was the normal pecking order of those days.

Rudder, in his great work, states that Queen Eddit held the manor and village which had fourteen hides, thirty-six villeins, thirteen bordar and eighteen servi.

This was quite a high number of slaves, so it must have been a bustling place long before the conquest.

Later on, the village was given a market but this was never highly popular. Market day was Tuesday and there were two fairs, on 24th May and 24th October. The charter for these was renewed in the reign of James I.

It had a bailiff as its chief officer who was chosen annually at the Court Baron before the lord or his chief steward. It was very important and one to which only freeholders had right of audience on civil matter. The bailiff would be attended by a sergeant at mace plus other officers.

One of their main and highly important functions was to examine all the weights and measures used by the trades people to stop blatant fraud. The bailiff also had authority to act as a peace officer.

Marshfield always thrived at making malt for Bath and Bristol. Once it must have been a frantically busy place.

The stage's arrival would be the highlight of the day, with passengers to attend to and the horse team to change.

Rudder speaks of three rocks which mark the boundaries of Gloucestershire, Wiltshire and Somerset. His book came out in the eighteenth century and the 'rocks' are referred to as very old, even then. They stand today, though need a little hunting. Now they are called The Three Shire Stones. They are not quite as gigantic as those of Stonehenge, although they are pretty large.

They have been erected on the same principle as the ones at Stonehenge, so must be unique in the area, rather like some primitive chieftain's tomb.

The countryside is gorgeous and from Marshfield a boy named Josiah Hort left his home to go to London at the end of the seventeenth century. He became a lifelong friend of Isaac Watts and rose to be archbishop. He was a profound scholar.

There is a lovely ancient tithe barn from about 1470, and almshouses of quite magnificent beauty. It is said that the outlying mansion now called The Tocks was once part of a Norman castle but, today, this is mere supposition.

What the village had in plenty, at one stage, were solid, stone cottages each of which had a shell porch over its front door. There are only a few left, but they are quite delightful.

It is supposed that Marshfield's industrial rival was Pucklechurch. Certainly, the latter village had a brisk, short-lived business at making felt hats with the usual deadly results for its workers.

Marshfield preferred to have nothing to do with that. Instead, it went in for making ladies' bonnets. In Victoria's day no lady worth her breeding would dream of going outside without a bonnet to protect her skin. Only the common and ill-bred had tanned or weather-beaten skin.

From The Crown, in High Street, it is possible to see the marker stone set into the pub's wall which states firmly it is 103 miles from this spot to Hyde Park Corner, London.

What is Marshfield like today? It is certainly not the bustling village it would have been in the days of stage-coaches and malt-making. It is a quiet village but it has retained remarkable olde worlde charm.

Probably the greatest objects to admire are the boundary stones. How many people see them when they whiz past in their cars? Antiquity is so often ignored in this twenty-first century. What a shame.

Miserden

The Slad valley of Gloucestershire is a truly delightful part of the County made famous by Lee's book *Cider with Rosie*. The land climbs slowly to form the backbone of the Cotswolds, the proper start of England's spine.

The views are out of this world without having the savagery of a mountain although it is unlikely the Romans were interested in any aesthetic appeal. They rarely went in for such frivolity when they lived in a strange land among well-known hostiles.

What they would have appreciated was the positive virtue of such landscape for their famous road-building. As far as they were concerned, this part of Albion was made to order for their road-building. Not that such communications were simply for X to send a herald to Y with a dinner invitation at X's villa. As always Rome's priority was an ability to move a fighting Legion fast and far to nip troubles in the bud, especially against the difficult and well-known bloody-minded Britons, who failed to appreciate Rome's occupation simply had to bring the natives nothing but benefits.

They went to town on the Cotswolds with the Fosse Way and Ermine Street to name but two and the former is not all that far from Miserden.

This little place had eighteen old names with many different spellings, which were nothing to do, apparently, with the Romans. Two of which are Musardera and Musardere yet before these names there was another known as Grenehamstede. It is thought the latter translates from the very Old English and means a place in a deep valley. This makes some historians state this is Miserden's only proper name. Actually Miserden comes down from that of the old dominant family of Musard and in the Old French this means stupid! The park is still known as Misardan Park.

It was all part and parcel of the Hundred of Biseleha. Domesdays tells us it had five bordars, eight villeins, one radchenistre and ten servie or slaves. Rather a lot of slaves for such a small place.

A bordar was someone who cultivated the land but was of an inferior status in life: what we might call today a little man with a tiny smallholding; not a farmer with many acres. A radchenistre had a much higher status in life because he was a freeman, which was of extreme importance in the pecking order of that time. Sometimes he might be called a riding man, which tells us he owned a valuable horse. A slave was nothing but a human animal with a value far below that of an ox.

We know very little about Miserden before Domesday except it was part and parcel of a manorial estate. The nearby Sudgrove settlement certainly dates from at least 1327. The whole was in the Wishanger Estate owned by the Knights Hospitaliers. This ancient order owned vast tracts of useful land.

There are several barrows in the area which tells us about pre-Roman times and how early man liked the region. Some have been opened for historical study and yielded skeletons which, after examination, have been decently interred again.

A noble by the name of Hascoit Musard came with William I from Normandy. He must have fought well and to William's approval because he was rewarded with huge estates, one of which included Miserden.

For some time this estate descended from son to son until it arrived at one Ralph. He was the Sheriff of Gloucester and married Isabel, the widow of John de Nevill. He did this without the King's licence which was most unwise because in those days monarchs could be very touchy and thin-skinned about what went on in their realms.

Ralph was forced to pay a fine of 100 marks for this sin, quite a considerable sum, so his lady must have had something about her with a vengeance. Who knows, it might even have been an extremely rare love match and not just an economic pact.

It is thought this Baron was one who built a castle in John's reign though it would not be a huge, stone construction like that at Windsor: more likely just a fortified building, probably made of timber; just something to keep the locals in order.

When Ralph died, his son Robert inherited, and he too must have ruffled regal feathers in some way because the castle and all the land was seized by the King, though this did not last long. It might just have been a royal tantrum though it is most unlikely Robert would have got his property back without a handsome backhander.

Down the line of sons it went until he it came into the hands of Hugh le Dispenser. This man was also attainted in the reign of Edward II and it was granted to the Earl of Kent, the youngest son of Edward I.

The next excitement becomes nothing but a list of head choppings until the reign of Edward II. The estate now went to Geoffrey Mortimer but he too had to part with his head at Smithfield. It seemed as if there was a gremlin brooding over the whole of this estate.

Some of this early history does become rather vague through gaps in old records but we do know that John of Woodstock died, seized of the estate and Elizabeth, his widow, held it in dower until her death in the reign of Henry IV.

Joan, commonly known as the Fair Maid of Kent, was John's heiress. Through her, the estate slowly worked its way down to Anne, sister and co-heiress of Edmund. Once again, it all passed into royal hands until the reign of Henry VIII.

Then we have the Kingston family on the scene but they soon sold to the Jernegans. For some odd reason, no one appeared to wish to hold this estate for any length of time. Perhaps many of these short-term owners were simply short of hard cash or worried more about keeping their heads on their necks after the estate's previous, gloomy history of beheadings.

Miserden became a very tiny place with only a handful of residents in it. In 1724 there were only twenty-four houses with a total population of 103. It was at this time that the fine Sudgrove House was constructed by the rector John Durston – a remarkably fine house which, in the twentieth century, became the home of the late Pat Smythe, famous show jumper and writer.

The Miserden village is all so pretty without being chocolate-boxy. There are the golden hills clad with huge wooded cliffs and slopes which glow against the blue and white sky. Completely unspoiled.

Miserden was never fated to grow either fast or big. It was far too dignified for that. By the mid-thirties of the twentieth century, the number of houses had shrunk to twelve cottages and two larger homes, one of which was Sudgrove.

There is a charming old church with a splendid lych gate though it is sadly in need of a lick of paint or preservative. It was from this church that the Reverend R B Earee, rector from 1890 until 1920, wrote his popular book. It became a standard textbook on postage stamp forgeries called *Album Weeds.*

On land not far away is another tiny place called Whiteway. This too has its claim to fame, which is rather unusual. In the early part of the twentieth century, a social experiment was tried. A small group of men and women from Surrey came across this hamlet. It was exactly that for which they were looking and they stayed to put down rather unusual roots.

Their idea of life was absolute self-sufficiency. A modern comparison could be the popular television series of *The Good Life.* These people made themselves into a commune based upon the tenets of Tolstoy.

The idea was they would look after themselves completely. No government help was wanted. No stuff called money. No postal services, police force or transport. No nothing at all.

That was a little high-faluting as they discovered very quickly. They found they had to make objects to sell for despised cash. They stuck to their original beliefs as best as they could and kept themselves very much to themselves.

In 1930 there was a radical change when a new generation

flexed its muscles and forced through a decision for majority voting at all meetings. Strangely enough, before World War II, Whiteway's children who did leave home would always return.

Matters had to change with the war as well as after it. Principles had to become more flexible. Even *The Goods* found it hard to pay their rates with eggs! Hard cash is vital in our modern society.

The commune exists today though much more watered down. These free-thinkers still keep themselves to themselves. From chatting to a resident, it appears most of the other villagers happen to hold the same opinion, It seems a little weird in this twenty-first century that a small country area can function under two such disparate ways of life.

Does it matter either? Just as long as the beautiful little area does not become marred with anything tatty or ugly.

Moreton in the Marsh

Moreton in the Marsh where the frogs croak harsh is the old doggerel about this Cotswold town. It is a very small town or an overgrown village, depending upon one's Cotswold taste. Probably almost half and half with the town part winning more often than not.

What is certain is that fantastic Roman Road, the Fosse, runs straight through the centre of Moreton and it deviates not one inch either.

The Marsh bit of the name is rather misleading. Visitors must drive up, look around and ask where all the wet ground is. Although Moreton is no Sahara, neither do the inhabitants have to wade constantly knee-deep in boggy ground. The real word should be March which means nothing more or less than a humble boundary.

Up until recent boundary changes made by local authorities and the government, there was a spot not far from Moreton which was unique in that it was the place where four Counties met. These were Gloucestershire, Oxfordshire, Worcestershire and Warwickshire. The precise place was called the Four Shires.

Like so many other places in England, Moreton has had a variety of old names in centuries gone by, twenty at a count and there are probably more if dialect is taken into consideration. For a very long time it was known simply as Morton Henmarsh.

It lay in the Hundred of Westminster in a vale with a ridge of hills on one side. From these, it is true, water flows freely but it certainly cannot be considered a pure marsh.

Moreton comes from the old meaning for moor or a lowish tract of ground. Henmarsh is roughly the same. Hen means old in this case and not poultry and *meanc* is just another word for limit or boundary so it is easy to work out today's modern name.

It is all dominated by the mighty Roman Road, the Fosse, which thunders dead ahead. There are two argumentative schools of thought about the road at this point. One swears that the ground really is *wet* and that the Romans needed to put down extra foundations. The other camp disputes this hotly and says through the middle of Moreton there is nothing but hard and dry earth.

It is certain Moreton was a tribal boundary for the ancient British tribes and these were of supreme importance. Like animals patrolling their territories so no tribe worth its salt would allow another to encroach. Tribute would have been demanded or weapons used without hesitation.

There would certainly have been skirmishing fights with the Romans but, in a set battle, the Britons had to lose. The Romans were simply better trained, more highly disciplined and extremely well led. Where the Britons could score was in guerrilla tactics on their small, native ponies – quick in-and-out harassing raids.

No matter how many fights there were, the Romans had come to stay so they consolidated their positions always with their road-building for rapid communications and troop movements. Villas, hot baths and all other appurtenances of their good civilisation had to join the queue until after the road-building had been completed.

Roman coins have been found, and not far away there are two barrows. The British tribe during the Saxon period would have been the Mercians with the northern fringe, the Hwicce paying tribute to them.

Land was given by Edward the Confessor to Westminster and this was to continue right down until 1830 when the manorial rights were bought by John Freeman, Baron Redesdale.

From the Domesday Book we know that Westminster held eight hides of land. A number of radchenisters lived there. Always freemen, they also ploughed, harrowed and reaped which tells us they were a most independent-minded lot; proud of their free status, but also willing to help out, if refusing to be pushed too far.

The abbots of Westminster must have kept a steady eye upon Moreton because they were constantly concerned about the tiny handful of inhabitants. They wished to make Moreton into a great place though their actual reasoning is quite unclear. Snob status?

In the reign of Henry IV the abbot procured a charter which totally exempted all the burgesses from paying tax in the four Counties. This was extremely valuable, as it would be with us today! We also know these burgesses were granted in fee simple and only had to pay a tiny fine if they were alienated or departed for pastures new.

This would be pretty unlikely. Most people spent their lives where they were born, especially the women folk.

Here was also a grant for a Court of Pleas for debts as well as one for criminal acts. Exactly how much this encouraged growth is unclear. It seems the great problem was that Moreton was just a little too near to other places of like stature.

Country people are well-known to be precise in their speech. A townie calls a sheep a sheep and that is that. In the Cotswolds they were referred to as tups, wethers or ewes. Just as the Moreton people called the Fosse Way the Stow Highway.

This was the place where Charles I was reputed to have lodged at the White Hart Inn on the night of the 2nd July 1644. It is said the nearby cottage hospital had, for a long time, the chair and footstool used by him.

In 1755 the famous road was turnpiked. It is thought a bridge, about then, was called the Kyte Bridge and stood at the northern end of the town. At the opposite, southern end, it was known simply as Stow Bridge.

During the Stuart epoch, Moreton fell upon hard times. The wool and its cloth trade had begun to vanish leaving many without work or hope. Before the end of the eighteenth century, the population had dwindled to 600 souls.

It was a Mr Busby who was responsible for changing matters a little. He bought the Manor House which dates from 1680 and is said to have bought it very cheaply. The reason given is that the house had a personal ghost. It was reputed to be haunted by Dame Creswyke, wife of a previous leaseholder.

Mr Busby must have hooted at this nonsense. He promptly redecorated right through and this seems to have put the ghost off her hauntings. Certainly she was never seen again. Perhaps this might be because Mr Busby used stones looted from the old Moreton church.

In the eighteenth century flax was grown in the district on its clay land. Mr Busby is responsible because work appeared again for the women and children. At one time there were forty-one linen weavers as well as those who worked from their own cottages.

Linen was made for coarse sewing and to make threads, cheesecloth and linseys. This last was a thin, rather crude cloth made from a mixture of linen, wool and inferior cotton.

By 1807 a lot of this work had also vanished though some women did continue to spin in the evenings for decades afterwards from their cottages.

The next great event to become 'the talk of the town' happened in 1826 when a horse tramway was opened between Moreton and Strafford upon Avon. There was a small side branch to Shipston on Stour in Warwickshire. Its main purpose was to take agricultural produce from Moreton and the surrounding district to Stratford and bring back coal. It ran for just sixteen miles to a navigable part of the River Avon. In its best days it was calculated it hauled 15,000 tons of coal annually.

From 1845 this tramway was leased to the Oxford, Worcester and Wolverhampton Railway and was altered in 1853. About this time the main railway line also started to run through Moreton. It took coaches and trucks from the main line.

Passenger traffic ceased in 1859 though the line remained open until 1881. In 1889 the track from Moreton to Shipston was converted for use by steam. During 1812 the Cheltenham and Cotswold Railway came before public notice. The Parliamentary bill for this was defeated and the company soon afterwards collapsed. It was found the directors were involved in some shenanigans and the nasty word of fraud was used.

It all arose because Sir George Wright with a rotative steam engine had, with others, cooked up an idea to cut water pipes for various sizes from solid stones. Huge quantities were sold in advance by the directors to the Manchester Water Works whose directors just happened to be those for the Stone Pipe Company. All neatly tied up together.

In this century the strength of steam engines was often disputed and their climbing and hauling abilities questioned and all this caused an uproar. Another lot of trouble rose from the Mickelton Tunnel. The owner of the land refused to sell. Whether he was being downright awkward, or had worked out his land's value and wanted more money, is rather unclear. He did eventually sell so the line could then run from Moreton to Honeybourne and Oxford.

So now we are down to the twenty-first century. Moreton still has a pretty good market even if there is not such a high volume of animals about. The Fosse continues to dominate by stabbing the heart of the town, and Moreton itself? It is a nice little place to visit or to take a break on a long drive north. There are a variety of fascinating shops for goods as well as for eats and about the town there is still a delightful olde worlde charm.

Oldbury on Severn

This little village has had a battery of old names which total eleven and two of which are Aldeburhe as well as Wolbery. All of them translate to mean an old fortification which is perfectly understandable taking into consideration the siting of the village.

There was a definite ancient and circular encampment built just north of the village and also a Roman one to the south about one mile distant. Both were built upon hillocks which rise out of the marshland which is inclined to sprawl from the edge of the mighty River Severn.

The great historian Atkyn says there was a regular passage over the river from Oldbury to Albon which was sometimes known as Aventon. He says that King Edward the elder stayed one time at Oldbury while Leoline, Prince of Wales, was at the other side. The King, no doubt pulling rank, invited the Prince to come over to him to treat for peace but Prince Leoline would have none of this. Obviously he must have been a much younger man and perhaps still stuffy with inflated dignity.

Edward showed he was more manly and kingly because he did not hesitate and promptly crossed over to the Prince. When Leoline realised what the King intended he must have been consumed with downright embarrassment because he ran into the water and carried the King back to his side of the shore on his back. He then said, "Your humility has overcome my pride!" and immediately did homage to the King.

The church occupies the site of the Roman Camp and its location is quite outstanding. There is a pull-up to the medieval north porch and from this position there is the most magnificent view of the river with the bridges to the left and the nuclear power station on the right. Straight over the water is the land of the commencement of the Forest of Dean.

There is a quaint legend as to how the site for the church was selected. The village people could not or would not agree as to where the church was to be built. Matters became more than a little heated and certainly unchristian. Finally one faction had its way and built the church elsewhere. It was destroyed at night so they built again with the same result. It is easy to imagine how the other half of the villagers must have chortled, "I told you so!"

Once more there were rows so an old hermit was consulted. He was recognised as a very wise man and he gave specific orders. The villagers were to yoke two maiden heifers together and let them wander at will. Where the heifers finally stopped would be the perfect place for the church and one not chosen by any man. It was a simple way to make a decision and halt further inter-village disputes.

So the villagers watched and off went the heifers. They wandered here and stepped aside there but kept going until, at the top of the steep hill, they decided enough was enough. They halted and made it clear they wished to be unyoked to graze more freely. Hence the site of the church was finally decided and no human blood shed in the process. It is a charming tale and it might even be true. We are in no position to dispute anything.

However, one legend can usually be matched by another. This one holds that Oldbury's patron saint was Alfrida. She was considered a most pious virgin who was foully murdered by a vicious tyrant called Munsius. If this second tale is the true one it can only be presumed this moral virgin obviously refused to part with her most treasured possession, preferring to die first.

In olden days rape could not only be a cruel sport but a right demanded and expected by some nobles under the *droit de seigneur*. If this tale is the true one we can only presume that Munsius might have well and truly regretted his action but too late in the day. Saint Alfrida was held to have a personal well somewhere at the rear of the village and it was supposed to have magnificent curative powers. It is thought this must have been somewhere on the Kingston or Littleton roads.

There was certainly considered to be some kind of religious order near to the cross roads and a nearby pond was known as The Stir. This suggests monks might have been around to keep fish in it. Earthworks on the village had the weird name of The Toot which is really an old Saxon word for a Lookout Post.

The Despensers, famous in the reign of Edward II, were seized of this manor and it is a fact that Eubulo le Strange and his wife Aleria levied a fine upon Oldbury to the Use of Hugh le Despenser when the Knights Templars were seized of Oldbury Manor in the reign of Edward III. Upon the dissolution of that Order, the manor was then granted to the Veals. After this family we have the Kemyses succeeding but an Inquisition found Roger Kemyses to be a lunatic. Some of the lands around Oldbury then went into the hands of the Abbey at Tewkesbury before they were granted to the Pert family.

At the time that Atkyns published his book there were fifty houses in Oldbury with 200 inhabitants of which a mere ten were freeholders.

In 1742 a deed was legally drawn up, signed, witnessed and sealed which stated that Oldbury church choir solemnly swore to attend their choir practice on Thursday at 7.00 p.m. There was a fine of two pounds in default – a hefty sum then. There was only one exception to this rigid ruling and it concerned two fishermen, Edward and Matthew Hunt, who would always be excused, 'if they obliged to be a'Cunnings Putts in the Severn'. The reason for this rigid regulation was brought about because the choir's singing in general was almost past bearing. However, salmon made the best excuse of all.

Perhaps the most famous salmon fishermen at Oldbury were John and Aaron Taylor. They could always catch fish and their prices for sale could range from five old pennies to ten shillings a pound.

The church of St Alfrida was involved in a most terrible fire in 1897 with shocking damage but luckily the fifteenth-century tower and medieval north porch survived and were retained in the rebuilding.

There is a wide range of rocks called the Whitsun Rocks which are uncovered at low tide. When it was decided a nuclear power station was to be built at this spot, there was a huge uproar. A dam had to be constructed around these rocks' edges which was to make the vital lagoon for the twice-daily tides to fill. All power stations must have water, especially those of nuclear capacity.

The trouble was that the building of this lagoon destroyed one of the very best salmon fishing spots on the whole river. There was fierce opposition but how can ordinary people hope to beat down a nuclear giant? The only redeeming point is that, like all nuclear power stations, great care has been given to the environment with nature walks, bird-watching stations and considerable attention paid to all the flora and fauna. There are excellent guided tours of the power station and, from the very top, a most stunning view of the river and the two bridges.

Today Oldbury is a gentle and tranquil village. The church still stands aloof from most of the houses and cottages. Inside, its design is simple, probably some might call very basic, yet it has immense dignity. The beautifully constructed roof with its crossed, supporting buttresses is magnificent and worthy of very detailed study.

Inside the ancient porch with its huge, solid door, there is a fascinating list, nicely framed. It gives the names of all the natural, indigenous flowers which can be found growing in the sloping church yard. There are just over one hundred.

Because of its elevation, this church does indeed stand four-square to all that which Nature throws at it – yet it has thrived for centuries. It dominates, appears to rule and makes a perfect place for visitors as the guest book just inside the door shows.

Pucklechurch

Pucklechurch has had a battery of names; sixteen at the last count, both before and after Domesday. Many start with the word pucel, which roughly means goblin. The connection with the village is a puzzle.

It was the seat of a royal Saxon palace for years. This would only be a large wooden building, but considered adequate for those days. Without proper maintenance though, it would soon rot away and vanish. Maps of the area suggest the palace's site, unexplored, is to the rear of today's Star pub.

It was here that King Edmund was murdered, probably by mistake. He was killed by a robber Leofa, whose name is also given as Leolf. This robber attempted to attack the king's steward Leon. When the king rushed down to intervene, he took a knife in the middle for his pains and quickly expired.

Recent research has uncovered two different stories as to what happened to Leofa then. The first and most natural is that the king's guards speared him to death. The second is that he made his escape. This sounds a little far-fetched but, upon a close examination of the known facts, becomes reasonable.

King Edmund had been celebrating the Feast of St Augustine, he who first preached the gospels to the Anglo-Saxons. After the scuffle which was fatal to the king, nobody did anything.

It was not that they did not care about their ruler, far from it. They were too confused, horrified and, at first, disbelieving. It is also most likely they were all blind drunk and incapable of either thought or action. This does have a ring of truth because the Anglo-Saxons liked their drink, especially when celebrating.

Leofa would, of course, have been promptly made an outlaw, which was a harsh punishment. Basically man is a herd animal, with a few exceptions made by natural loners. Certainly in the first millennium, as for centuries even before, men clustered together because they had need of each other's help and skills in the matter of simply surviving, especially in the winter months.

As the name implies, outlaw means just that. An outlaw was cast out from society. He could never get help, a bite of food or warmth. He had to live by himself in the wilds – and it was wild then. More important was the fact that the world outlaw meant the man was totally beyond the law. Anyone could kill him with total impunity. They would probably be suitably rewarded as well for the slaying of a regicide.

So, what happened to Leofa we have no idea. He most likely died alone one winter, hungry, frozen and miserable. He might have been killed by a bear before hibernation or a pack of starving wolves. He was never heard of again.

It seems the inhabitants of Pucklechurch must have been a rather difficult lot. They were allowed to glean wood, fruits and nuts from the forest. They took more than they should and were fined by the lord of the manor.

Many ancient roads passed through the area as well as a turnpike road from Wiltshire to Mangotsfield. There were also traces of a Roman road from Bath to Oldbury. All have long since vanished.

The lord of the manor arranged a market to be held on Wednesdays. Lords liked markets because they profited nicely from the trade. Pucklechurch people did not like this market, though. They refused to use it and did their buying and selling elsewhere, to the lord's fury. So he fined them. He also exacted a money penalty because they went in for usury, talked to those with leprosy and even had the gall to marry without his permission. One even sued a tenant with a king's writ in the lord's own court. No, the villagers were not frightened by feudal tactics. They would do their own thing.

At one stage, felt hats were made in the village. This would have been a small cottage industry and a dreadful, lethal occupation. Felt can only be made under certain conditions. There must be great heat and moisture, so windows were tiny. The rooms in which the work took place would have been a very fertile breeding ground for tuberculosis. At the same time, there was the hazard of using highly poisonous mercuric nitrate in the felt production.

Mercury poisoning is terrible. It inflames the membranes of the mouth, loosens the teeth and gives pain and also numbness and tremors in the extremities. There is both loss of weight and appetite. Worst of all, it affects the brain. People lost their marbles. It is exactly from this dangerous occupation that the saying has come down to us: 'As mad as a hatter!'

Like most of the region, Pucklechurch has coal. That which is found in the village area is black and highly bituminous. A lot of the poorest inhabitants obtained their bread by working for the coal master at the local colliery. This pit was only one of the enormous Bristol coalfields, worked as early as 1223.

With industry's arrival, though, coal sprang into its own and the village colliery did well – initially. Although not paid as well as those south of Bristol, the men could earn better than average for the local money. An adult collier earned eighteen shillings to £1 per week in full work and even a boy under thirteen years was able to take home two shillings to six shillings, figures hard to translate with decimalisation and inflation.

It was good, reliable money while it lasted. At one stage, the village and surrounds had twenty-one working collieries, but by 1900 the number had dropped down to eleven. Twenty years later there were only five, then none at all.

Most of the trouble came from water and the pumping necessary to keep the headings open for the workers. With the death of the coal-mining industry, Pucklechurch sank back into village life.

Just before the pits closed, though, there was a quarry which produced a coarse kind of black marble used a lot for chimney pieces and gravestones. Gradually this industry too faded away.

In the latter part of the twentieth century a remand prison was opened.

A fairly large trading estate grew so what do we have today? A quiet little village with a sprinkling of new houses and nothing really to indicate its historical past.

Perhaps there is a kingly ghost roving around somewhere?

Rangeworthy

Rangeworthy is one of those rare places which does not have a mention in the Domesday Book. The reason is that it came under the Thornbury Hundred. There were forty-two villagers and fifteen slaves in a hundred which comprised seven other villages. So Rangeworthy was considered too small for a mention. The first time it comes to light properly is in the thirteenth century when Thornbury is divided into an Upper and Lower Hundred.

This does not mean Rangeworthy was a nonentity place. Far from it. It had, like all other villages and towns, an interesting variety of names. There is Rengeswuda, Rengew, Rendworthe and Rungewurthy. It is thought that the word 'ringe' meant a tub and 'renge' tells of a range or row. There is a possibility they could mean filled wood, brushwood or just a parcel of land.

Before William I it was held by the Saxon Earl Brictric who had vast holdings in today's South Gloucestershire but he lost the lot to William's wife Matilda when he spurned her in matrimony.

Patch Elm Lane is well-known today and this name may have come from Patisplace because that is what is recorded as long ago as 1388. Strangely enough in 1413 this name had altered to Patyesnelme. This mediaeval English could only mean the place of an elm tree or simply be someone's name. We will never really know.

After the conquest an early owner was Hugh de Audley, Earl of Gloucester but in 1333 a rich freeman by the name of William Borough came on the scene. He was also given custody of Eastwood Park from one John Mostel.

In this period some interesting facts can be found regarding parkers. He was a person of some importance locally and in 1327 his wage was 2d per day which went up to the dizzy sum of 3d per day in 1332.

This sum seems ridiculous to us yet it was of enormous importance for one great reason. It was always there and guaranteed. Even a bailiff only earned 4d per day.

The social status of both men was much lower than that of a chief steward, treasurer or general receiver who were usually knights of the realm.

By 1546 Sir Nicholas Poyntz was on the scene but only for a while. He had to surrender the estate to the king because he was in arrears of rent. So the area continued in the hands of the crown until King James granted it, free of rent, to Sir William Whitmore.

The next figure upon Rangeworth's scene was a remarkable man of importance to the whole country. Sir Matthew Hale bought it for £1,000, a huge sum of money. He was supposed to pay this off in six months but he was ten days late in raising the final £125.

Sir Matthew Hale was of Magdalen Hall, Oxford, and Lincoln's Inn. He became counsel in law during the civil wars for a number of people against General Fairfax. Yet he also tendered his services to Charles I. He took the oath to the Commonwealth but then defended Christopher Love.

He was a giant of his times and obviously highly respected by both royalists and parliamentarians. He was knighted in 1660, became Lord Chief Justice in 1671 with a seemingly crammed full legal life. Yet he had time to show a great interest in a house.

Rangeworthy Court was probably built somewhere around the twelfth century and must have been for some lord of the manor. Sir Matthew leased the property to his son, another Matthew, but he died in 1675 without leaving a will. What he did leave were a pile of debts instead.

Rangeworthy Court with its rare extended collar roof was then doomed to lead a rather chequered life for a time. It is known it was leased as a farmhouse during the nineteenth century and suffered enormous neglect.

It was not until well into the twentieth century that Rangeworthy Court would be tactfully restored to its former glory. During the Second World War it was again bought by a successful farmer. He simply kept the land and working buildings, then sold the house. For a while it was a school, but about twenty-five years ago it became a hotel.

While all this was going on, Rangeworthy still tended to be under Thornbury's thumb. In 1801 only 230 people lived there and a century later the population had only increased by exactly nine.

In 1882 there was reported in the *Bristol Mercury* a very large meeting held at the Swan Inn, Thornbury. The object of this exercise was to elect a mayor after a satisfactory dinner had been eaten.

Juries were then sworn in and officers elected. They were officers of the borough, the mayor, the sergeant at mace, constables, ale tasters, searchers and sealers of leather and carnals. The latter word is highly intriguing without further explanation.

It must all have ended upon a very convivial note because once these men, no women of course, had been chosen, they all retired to the mayor's house and obviously it was not for a simple chat. It is easy to imagine the ale consumed.

For many years, going right back to the seventeenth century, coal had been obtained from this area. The early colliers were not great believers in making maps so it is difficult to indicate their workings.

An old shaft is shown within spitting distance of today's Rangeworthy Court in one map but with no further explanation. Rangeworthy Colliery itself, also known as the Old Wood Colliery, was sited very roughly near the end of Tanhouse Lane. It was 450ft deep and passed through several seams above and below the well-known Hard Vein. Old workings could well have existed in what was called the Little Vein, but there are no records at all.

In 1890 a surveyor's report stated the seam was two to three feet thick and the coal to be inferior and almost unmarketable. Another opinion much later in 1945 reported this coal was excellent and in large lumps. It appears trouble was caused by too many officials. The old story of too many chiefs and not enough Indians. It is also reported the company undertook an Admiralty contract they simply could not fulfil.

Finally, when the Yate collieries closed, the death knell was also sounded for Rangeworthy pit.

Another prime reason was that Old Wood received too much water. Pumping was a never-ending battle, not just for coal cutting, but men's lives. In certain areas around Rangeworthy the coal comes to the surface and displays itself as a peculiar grey earth.

This is most noticeable down at Lower Common. Strictly speaking this is the last piece of land in Yate yet Rangeworthy has always flexed its muscles and considered Lower Common belonged to it. It's not easy to grow produce at Lower Common simply because of this soil. The writer lived there and speaks from frustrated experience.

So, like many other apparently boring or even humdrum

villages in our area, Rangeworthy too has had its share of history.

There have long been rumours that the Romans also liked this particular area. One of the farming families had, for years, been turning up unusual artefacts and storing these in their loft. The Hill End Farm acquired quite an unusual collection of brooches, pins, dice and coins.

Finally a dig was started which produced astounding results. Instead of one villa, which had been suspected, the historians found they had discovered the site of a long-lost town probably built somewhere around the first century. This was no small effort either because it gave information that thirty-seven acres had been made into a fortified town complete with city gates, a civic meeting point and well-defined streets, a smelting works and many houses.

It was suggested this might even have been a regional capital, a centre for both trade and industry all of which would have been under the alert and watchful eye of Old Sodbury Fort. Just a short, brisk horse ride away were the fighting men of the Legion, under, initially, the short tempered, aggressive Publius Ostorius Scapula, Governor of Britain, who had little love for the Britons in the first place.

As this dig progresses, much more will be learned of this remarkable town which has been hidden for nearly two thousand years. Nothing is ever quite what it seems because our history lies just below the surface. It simply awaits discovery.

River Severn

The world's longest river is the Nile with a massive 4,090 miles to its credit. The incredible Amazon nearly reaches this length but also has a quite incredibly wide mouth and delta. In comparison, the River Severn appears almost miniscule yet it has its own claim to fame even if it is only about 180 miles long because nothing is really what it seems.

The Severn's traits and foibles give it fame in its own right as well as notoriety. To start with, it has the second highest rise and fall of the tide anywhere in the world. It has an impressive and mesmerising Bore and it is not a river to be trifled with. At certain times when the moon, tides and winds collaborate, the tide can come in and rise at the speed of a fast moving horse.

The Severn or in Welsh, the Harfen, is this country's greatest tidal river. Its birthplace is near to the River Wye on the slopes of Plynlimon in Wales and it then follows a semi-circular course towards the Bristol Channel and the Atlantic Ocean. It drains a large area amounting to 4,350 square miles and during its travel it descends from 2,000 feet at its source down to 500 feet at Llanidloes. It gradually travels lower until it floods into the Bristol Channel.

It was during the Ice Age we call the Pleistocene that the waters could only escape through Ironbridge because of the thick ice and this course was that which continued after the Ice Age vanished. The river becomes tidal as high up as Gloucester and becomes a force with which to be reckoned. A wise person does not take the Severn lightly – if they wish to continue living. This river is perfectly capable of killing.

In 1606 the river went manic. On a January day a massive wall of water was seen approaching and some accounts say it was as high as the churches' towers. This was far more lethal than any Bore. Some few who managed to survive likened it to hills of water which moved with such incredible speed, even the birds could not escape. The loss of life to man and animals was appalling.

There was no warning at all as the water stormed over the defences to crash and flood twenty parishes. Even urban areas to the south like Bristol and Minehead were invaded. Possibly the very worst affected areas were in the Berkeley Vale from Sharpness up to Frampton. In less than two hours life as it was then known, changed with hundreds, perhaps even thousands drowning and there were no emergency services then.

Many died afterwards from sheer hunger and disease while homes and even villages were swept away as the farmland flooded. People clung to church steeples until they dropped from exhaustion and cold. No one will ever really know how many did die. And the loss of precious livestock was catastrophic for people who did not have much in the first place.

The cause? This is still unknown though historians have dismissed both an earthquake and tsunami. It may have arisen from an extremely rare combination of a storm in the Atlantic, flooding from a sudden snow-melt on the higher land plus a very high tide. Whatever the cause was, this one day in 1606 caused untold misery, destruction and death to so many. Can it ever happen again? Who knows??? (See 'The Noose'.)

The river is infested with mud flats, quick sands, whirlpools and exceedingly dangerous currents. Its speed can be awesome, its sheer power ferocious. All past bridge builders have had to deal with enormous problems especially when the two bridges were constructed in 1966 and 1996. When the early bridge was opened by Her Majesty it was the second longest river bridge overall and its construction pioneered procedures which were new. These included an aerodynamically shaped deck with leaning suspension hangers. The second bridge became the longest overall in the country which also included the very longest cable staying span.

Huge caissons had to be sunk inside of which men worked, always with one nervous eye on the tide. Small craft were anchored permanently nearby when men were down in the caissons or even in their vicinity.

The mighty strength of the currents gave tremendous stress problems which had to be calculated to the nth degree by the civil engineers and there was a similar problem when the cables were due to be spun. When the wind comes from a particular quarter the forces exerted against bridges are awesome. So the second, newer bridge has been able to remain open even under extreme weather conditions because of its wind shielding. Sometimes though the earlier bridge has had to be closed against the violent turbulence.

The Severn's estuary widens considerably between South Wales and Somerset and it is this which makes the famous Bore. The dictionary definition of any Bore is 'a tidal flood which rushes up the estuaries of certain rivers also called an eagre'. The Severn's Bore is geographical in design with a generous dollop in its recipe from weather and lunar cycle.

The Bristol Channel is rather like a very wide-mouthed funnel. The actual neck of this funnel though is a very thin taper which does not always run straight and true. It can twist and turn very violently. At the same time, the floor of the river is unusual in that it rises and falls just like a switchback. Its levels are totally erratic and quite unexpected to the unwary. It can rise vertically then suddenly plunge down almost like a lift shaft.

Such violent contortions affect water's flow. The freshwater which is constantly coming down the river from the higher land is often coupled with a strong wind. This can delay or even advance the predicted time of the Bore's arrival at any one of the favoured viewing points.

The High or Spring tides can occur on several days in a lunar month and they may last for a few days. But this does not mean each day will produce the Bore. The height of the Bore can vary enormously depending upon all of these given factors. It has been known for the Bore to reach a height of two metres and move at about ten miles an hour.

But how, people ask, puzzled? Water flows down the river. The tide comes in. The two meet and collide with the more powerful, at that moment, assuming supremacy. The waves then simply override the downwards-flowing water to proceed upstream as a giant wave. So at the time of the Bore, the river's water is really flowing in two directions at once; down as well as upstream and something has to give which makes the Bore.

This famous Bore attracts people from all points of the compass but prudence should be the order of the day. It is wise to arrive at the chosen viewing spot early as hundreds of other people have exactly the same idea. Some of the best viewing spots are at Over Bridge, Stonebench and Minsterworth. At the latter place, people must keep to the river banks because much of the adjoining land and roads are private.

For those who are young and more daring, the Bore becomes the ideal challenge to be viewed afloat. There are certain, rather obvious rules to be followed for safety's sake. Observation of the normal river speed limit and certain power craft must *not* go through the Bore as this action ruins the spectacle for those on the river bank.

Spectators at Stonebench should be even more cautious because the Bore's arrival is often not the end of the entertainment. Far from it. The river can surge enormously *after* the Bore has gone on its merry way upstream with the result that flooding often takes place. It is not at all unknown for spectators to have to be rescued and it does not require much imagination to guess what happens to the various cars around.

This river demands respect in all of his moods because, in a kind of casual manner, it is very much a killer.

St Briavels

Domesday is quite clear that this name did not exist when the great record was compiled for William I. As it was near to Lydney it was called Little Lydney in the Hundred of that name. Before 1066 it was held by Alfhere and it had six hides which all paid tax. The population can only be described as miniscule with just three villagers, five smallholders plus three slaves. It is possible Lydney, sometimes spelled Lidney, came from the Old British word Llydan which described that broad part of the River Severn and Rudder says the 'ey' means a watery situation.

Later on though we have St Briavels with a huge variety of spellings numbering sixteen in total. Some historians argue this came from the name of a Welsh Saint called Briafael who had the baptismal name of Brioc or Brieuc. This is thought to be an early Welsh personal noun which gives us a possible source.

At this point, in much earlier times, the river was very broad indeed. The historians dispute hotly the reason for this width narrowing but it is likely this was a natural phenomenon over a long period because the great river has always had its violent moods. It certainly provided excellent pasturage for horses and cattle and, after a long winter, many horses were sent to rest and recover on such rich land. The river could run very high. So much so, Rudder thinks that, at one stage, the tide would rise to just within the churchyard and that a ship was built adjacent to this.

The earth has always been very rich in iron ore and pit coal as well as red and yellow ochre plus limestone and fossils. It is even rumoured that, long ago, the grinders of an elephant were found.

Probably an early notable resident was Milo, the Earl of Hereford who built the castle in 1164 and by then the little place was called St Briavels and not Little Lydney. One argument holds this comes from St Breakstone, one mile north of the castle's site. Although not gigantic by castle standards it was in a superb defensive position and easy to defend as well as being most difficult to storm. There was a splendid view with natural defences.

Milo did not live out a long life to enjoy his security because he was killed in a hunting accident on Christmas Eve in 1164 at Flatly. Whether this was genuine or an attempt to remove him, like the fate suffered by William II (Rufus), will never be known. Arrows fired by skilled archers were silent in their lethal abilities. Milo was certainly a man of consequence because he was the King's Officer and the Constable in charge of the Royal Wood and it is easy to imagine the uproar caused by his death though history is silent on details.

During the castle's construction remains were found of an old Roman encampment. These discoveries were reinforced when Mr Bathhurst built his magnificent seat about one mile from the church. Mr Bathhurst was also acutely aware of the rich earth because he had a large furnace for smelting the iron ore as well as several forges for manufacturing iron.

There were many old Roman coins as well as part of a tessellated pavement unearthed and Rudder confirms that, after rain, he too, found pieces of urns and fine, old pottery shards. Perhaps all these came from the Second Roman Legion?

One notable owner of the castle in the century was Anne of Warwick, daughter of the 14th Earl who came into the whole estate through inheritance. Then she had problems. After the death of her husband on the field at Barnet, his estate was confiscated because he had taken up arms against Richard II and was attainted. For the devious purpose of securing the whole estate for the brothers of the royal victors at Tewkesbury, a Council solemnly stated she was officially dead. When Henry VII came to the throne this ridiculous decree was annulled as 'against all reason'. However, matters were not quite what they seemed. No sooner was the lady in possession again than the King demanded she show by what right she did indeed now hold them! Probably tired of all this hassle and knowing she had no chance of victory against a King, the unfortunate lady took the only sensible course of action. She granted the whole estate to the King for himself and his heirs forever.

The castle then had rather a chequered history. It was a hunting lodge, a court and even a prison, especially for debtors, and it held the two latter functions well into the mid-nineteenth century. The Youth Hostel opened in 1948 and was popular from the start as it made an ideal base for exploration of both the

Gloucestershire Way as well as Offa's Dyke Path. It has certainly come a long way over the centuries since constructed.

In the village there is the George Inn built in the seventeenth century and St Mary's Church which is much older. Visitors might be amused at the written request to 'Close the door to keep the birds out!' yet this church gives a personal history lesson at times. Its south side is Norman and erected around about 1089 though other parts date from two centuries later.

The famous bread and cheese ceremony is said to have started centuries ago though the first written record appears to be that of 1779. After evensong, on the old Whit Sunday, bread and cheese were handed out to the parishioners in an early kind of food parcel. It was also held to indicate their ancient feudal rights of woodcutting from Hudnalls Wood.

Unfortunately there were times when good manners were lacking because sometimes the preacher would be pelted with the food so in the mid-nineteenth century it was held outside the church. Then the inevitable happened and people turned up from all points of the compass for their freebies! There were deplorable scenes of people scrambling for the food, drunkenness and even worse, everyone quite prepared to fight to get their share.

This ancient ceremony was conducted for a number of generations by members of the Creswick family and the people held it all in high esteem for many years, like so many of these ancient customs though, this has gradually declined. It has lost any ability to fit into the twenty-first century which, perhaps, is rather sad. Even though cheeses are plentiful at supermarkets perhaps it is wrong to stand apart from old customs which all form our heritage.

This little community is a history book, a microcosm, and should be cherished as part and parcel of our national inheritance.

Sharpness

Sharpness had always nestled, cheek by jowl, with big sister Berkeley less than three miles to the south. Northwards there have also been close relations with the small villages of Hinton and Purton.

Many visitors think Sharpness, with its modern docks and smooth canal, to be very modern yet, like so many English habitations, it is ancient. It is pretty certain the ancient Britons were perfectly capable of crossing the River Severn in their flimsy coracles when the tide and weather conditions were right.

The whole of this area was once the Forest of Horwood which extended right down to Bristol. It was all felled and cleared when Hardinge, the Reeve of Bristol, became Lord of Berkeley.

Yet Sharpness does not seem to have had many ancient names. Only six can be found, one of which is the tongue twister of Schobbenasse. Scobba was another, which in the Old English simply means a headland.

Hinton has done better and boasts nine previous names, two of which are Hinith and Henton. The records say these mean a farmstead of a household but whose, we have no idea.

Purton's old names number merely three, the most popular of which seems to have been Piriton. A translation tells us this is a pear tree orchard or farm.

There are other old records and legends which refer to Hinton as Oldminster for the area now referred to as Newtown. At the same time, sometimes the name of Ness was used which simply adds to the general muddle.

We do know the Danes used the modern name because to them it was apt to describe the headland where the river narrows for some distance before it broadens again at Purton.

In 910 the Danes, always brilliant seamen and filled with natural belligerence, sailed up the Severn with their eyes wide open for loot, rape and plunder in general. For some time they made their homes at Sharpness but always kept one wary foot on their longboats with the other only balanced on the land.

They rampaged mercilessly, as was their wont. They never failed to return to Sharpness unless laden with booty. They became the terror of the region. On one occasion though it all went badly wrong for them. The Mercians, themselves hardly a pushover, were livid at the Danes' mayhem on their territory. There was a pitched battle at Cambridge, just north of today's Berkeley, then a tremendous slaughter at Wanswell.

The Danes were forced to take a very heavy defeat, something to which they were most unaccustomed. Rather subdued, with their numbers heavily decimated, they hastily departed.

Sharpness itself is made with an island between the river and today's canal though it was the river that dominated. We do know that Roger de Berkeley claimed a 'castellulum' at Ness, part of which now appears to lie under today's docks.

Domesday says that William FitzOsborn, the Earl of Hereford, took five hides of land at Ness and built himself a fortress with royal permission. This was sometime between 1067 and 1071.

Long before this time though, the region became connected to a rather strong-willed lady called Ciolburga. She was a widow and King Kenulf made her the abbess of the area and it can only be presumed she must have lived at or near to Berkeley.

It was not at all unusual in those days for a female to head a house of monks. Indeed it was not even considered essential for the lady to be a religious or to have taken vows.

In 804 though, it is held that Ciolburga met problems. Her son Ethelric secured, for her use only, other property in today's Westbury and Stoke. The official reason given was that this would 'provide her, during her lifetime, protections against the contentions of the local people'. Such a statement is tantalising so there must be a presumption the locals went in for bigotry and anti-sexuality.

The lady died in 807 but the Abbey held fast to her lands

and it was not until 824 when Heabert, Bishop of Worcester, finally managed to grab complete possession. There is apparently no mention of any abbess or nuns though 210 priests are reputed to have witnessed this thieving settlement.

Land was the most important commodity to own in those days and heads could roll quite easily concerning ownership if anyone tried to make a stand. It is not until 883, under King Alfred, that the situation finally appears to have been resolved. How much of this tale is factual is questionable but it makes a nice legend to hand down.

It is all supposed to have ended up in the ownership of Earl Godwin who promptly gave the lot to his wife. Why? No Inland Revenue claims to dodge in those days. Perhaps he was simply being astute and hedging his bets against kings changing their minds.

Godwin must have regretted his act because his wife is said to have refused to eat anything 'from that manor' on account of the Abbey's destruction. Destroyed by whom? Godfrey himself had to have had an excuse to snatch the land?

Some historians refute the idea there was an abbess or nuns in that area and that it was the Danes who destroyed everything in sight. Knowing the Danes' great joy at leaving ruins in their wake this is quite possible. Others say Godwin and his wife are but figments of somebody's vivid imagination. We will never know.

What is known positively is that in 1066 the owner of it all was Rex the King. After Hastings it belonged to William I, winner takes all, and who was there to deny him his right by virtue of conquest?

After 1066 the region simply drifted along its watery existence yet it still held fascination for royalty. In 1605 King James I visited the low-lying land near to Purton. He was attracted by the fact that, at certain times of the year, the low land opposite Slimbridge could be as much as three miles wide.

Yet conversely, at low tides, fishermen have always waded out with their lave nets but they have to know the threatening river very well. They must also have considerable respect for it. The River Severn is an 'unforgiving beast' and those who do not pay respect quickly die. There are quicksands and the tides come in very fast indeed.

There is a legend that, for a short time, Sir Walter Raleigh lived at Purton's manor but, again, facts are difficult to verify.

For innumerable centuries, men have sailed these highly dangerous waters. Particularly well-known were the Severn barge and trow men. They would sail from Sharpness up to Gloucester, all of twenty-six miles. A good crew could manage this in two hours especially when the bore was in their favour.

They used oars and pulled incredible weights as they were often laden with stone from Chepstow. Sometimes they were towed by a boat. It was quite normal for them to carry half a ton of stone as ballast.

As long ago as the eighteenth century men had talked about making a canal to shorten the distance to Gloucester and to make this an inland port. It would be designed to take sea-going ships right into the heart of Gloucester. Such a canal would be the then world's largest.

Between 1784 and 1793 four surveys were carried out, the last by Robert Mylne. It was he who took the first positive steps. By an Act of 1793 it was decided to make a canal 17.75 miles long. The capital cost of which was estimated to be £140,000. Mylne thought this should be £121,329.10.4d. This was a farcical figure, every bit as ludicrous as that given for building the London Dome, which needed constant injections of lottery money.

Work did begin in 1794 and it heralded the start of one of the world's most troubled canals to build. Mylne was eventually sacked though retained as a consultant.

By 1799 over £112,000 had been spent and yet the canal had only reached Hardwicke. In 1804 there was a scheme to raise an extra £110,00 by, of all things, a lottery but this idea was vetoed by William Pitt.

Another Act did manage to scrape up £80,000 but six years later only £50,000 of this had appeared. There was a fresh review in 1810-1811 with new, far more practical estimates. In 1817 the Committee pressed the work ahead to Sharpness.

The general financial situation changed for the better with the Poor Employment Act of 1817, which encouraged general loans to relieve unemployment.

On the 15th July 1818 the foundation stone was laid at Sharpness and work resumed again. The Commissioners advanced another £65,000. The connection was made to the Stroudwater Canal and, in 1820, the first real traffic was able to move. It was twenty-five years after the work had begun.

Then work stopped yet again with the plaintive cry that more money was wanted. £268,000 had already been spent so there had to be another loan of £60,000. Even three years later, when almost finished, the Commissioners were forced to lend another £30,000.

Then on the 26th April, 1827, the ship *Anne* of Bristol used the canal for the first time. The entire canal had cost the stupendous sum of £432,000 and had taken thirty-three years to build.

The next worry arose because the Commissioners threatened to sell all unless they were repaid their money promptly. Finally in 1850, the debt was settled by the simple expedient of borrowing from the Pelican Life Insurance Company. It was not until 1871 that all debts were finally cleared.

Initially there were great problems with a water source, which meant another Act for this to be sorted out. In a survey of 1869 the canal had been made big enough for sailing ships but it was too small for coastal steamers. More problems to be resolved, which they were in due course.

In 1874 there was a new docks entrance and the canal was in great use. There was a division of the canal and tidal lock gates at Sharpness.

In the nineteenth century, it also became very obvious that a railway bridge was also needed. In 1872 the Severn Bridge

Company was incorporated to construct a railway bridge over the river. The contract was let in 1875 to Hamilton Windsor Iron Works of Liverpool for £193,000.

Work started on the Sharpness side where the currents were weak. Cylinders were sunk and compressed air forced into them to thrust out the water. So sinkers could work on the bottom, often seventy feet below the waterline. Stages were then built, platforms made and spans erected. In the centre though the scaffolding was not strong enough for the sinking of the cylinders and Spring tides washed it all away.

The tidal rise is thirty feet in two and a half hours and the contractors were most up to date because they used the new-fangled electrical lighting at night.

The bridge was a series of iron bow girders which rested upon cast iron piers each of which was filled with concrete and rock. The total length, including the viaduct, was 4,162 feet. The total height from the deepest foundation rock was 150 feet.

For technically minded readers' interest, other facts are the water's headway was seventy feet. The iron used weighed in at 7,000 tons. The length of the spans was 327 feet for two of them. There were five of 171 feet and fourteen of 124 feet plus one span of 196 feet.

This remarkable bridge was opened on the 17th October 1879, just one hundred years after the first iron bridge was built over the Severn at Iron Bridge.

A first-class coach and salon were attached to the train at 10.15 a.m. from Bristol to Berkeley Road and two coaches on a special train from Gloucester. There were 400 people aboard. This meant the train now had twenty first-class coaches and salons to travel to Lydney.

As the train passed over the bridge it fired a twenty-one gun salute because a detonator had been placed on each of the twenty-one spans. After a brief stop at Lydney, the special returned to Sharpness but stopped before the bridge so people could get out, walk over and marvel.

The final grand total for this construction was £400,000, a staggering sum then, and the actual opening was performed by the Earl of Ducie.

This became a highly popular way to reach Lydney and it seemed it must go on for ever. Then disaster struck. Oddly enough it happened in the same month of October in 1960 and became sheer terror and death.

Two tankers called the *Arkendale* and *Wasdale* collided in dense fog. They burst into flames after an explosion at the bridge's base. It was enormous and brought down one of the bridge's main supports as well as two of the intermediate spans. A gap was left over 100 yards wide.

The railway track fell onto both blazing vessels which were carried by the Severn's currents to beach near Sharpness on a sandbank.

At this time, the bridge carried five trains daily in each direction plus a number of freight trains. By the grace of God none were in the vicinity at this time.

Five men died. Five families were devastated. The disaster now meant a thirty-mile road journey through Gloucester to reach the other side. Plans were made to rebuild the bridge but this never took place. There was total demolition of the remains, which started in August 1967 and by the summer of 1968, the bridge had gone for all time.

Sharpness's docks were enlarged in 1874. The tidal basin is 546 feet long and the floating dock covers about twenty acres in total. There are considerable dry-dock facilities, warehousing and many silos.

At this point the Severn is 1,200 yards wide but large ships cannot get any higher up the river because the deep-water channel ends. The very largest ships to enter the docks are of 3,000 metric tonnes. English tons are not used because with metric there is a higher fee; astute and thrifty.

Most of the ships carry dry cargoes, which range from cat litter, of all things, to all agricultural products and cement.

Ships from all over the Baltic and Europe as well as the eastern Mediterranean countries like Greece and Turkey use the port. The most important cargo is considered to be that of cement which usually arrives from Spain.

It is a complicated passage for ships to make and skilled pilotage is compulsory for all ships over a certain length times the beam. It is still very tricky to bring a ship in and the pilots must be first class because of the tides and currents.

There used to be a training ship for boys who wished to join the Merchant Navy to learn the skills of seamanship.

The utmost maximum length and beam advertised for canal boats is sixty-four metres long and ten metres beam. These are the measurements which have been tried and tested over many years. However, if an importer wishes to start and make regular runs with a larger ship, tests are carried out and a feasibility study conducted.

There was a local school in the early 1900s as well as the Great Western Railway for the inhabitants.

Many decades ago a lot of ships came in from Norway carrying timber. In due course, they erected a small church. After a time this was demolished and replaced with a fine brick one. It has a delightful tiled roof with some very unusual fancy exterior decorations. There was also a graveyard for the locals to use when their number came up.

Years ago the church was deconsecrated and initially turned into a transport yard. Today it holds a small car repair business but a peep inside shows the building still maintains its majesty. Outside the decorations are still in place for general admiration.

Not all that far from the church, at the end of Great Western Road, there is an old coastguard station with an adjoining picnic area, which gives a superb view of the Severn.

There is a lifeboat station at Sharpness under the Severn Area Rescue Association. There are two official rescue stations with the second sited at Beachley.

To some people, Sharpness today might seem nothing but a

mishmash of concrete facilities for ships yet it echoes our history. Man is not at all new here but he is certainly very puny compared to the might of the vicious River Severn.

Slimbridge

Unlike many other villages in Gloucestershire, Slimbridge has very few old names, and those which it does have give no explanation for their meaning. Even the great historian Rudder passes comment on this fact and states the name as shown in Domesday is written as Hislinbruge. Whether this name comes from the old German or the old Norse is highly debatable.

What is certain is that the area belonged to the Berkeleys and at that time of Domesday, it was held by Roger. He had the Lordship of ten ploughs as well as hides in numerous other small places. Doomsday though is positive that there were thirteen villagers, twenty-one smallholders as well as sixteen slaves. It also had a mill worth five shillings, quite a considerable sum for that time. Whether the mill was used for grinding corn, making cloth or alcohol is again not explained.

The land around this village has always been low lying, marshy and prone to flooding when the River Severn was in one of its erratic moods. The pasture land itself was good for the stock and considered valuable, although a prudent eye had to be kept upon the foibles of the powerful river.

There was a large tract of land call of the Dumballs, but more commonly known as the New Grounds. This consisted of about 1,000 acres, which had been gained from the river many years ago and which belonged to the Earl of Berkeley, because his manor extended down to the middle of the river.

During the time of King Charles I his Attorney General commenced a suit in the Exchequer against Lord Berkeley for exactly that portion of land. After the jury was empanelled and the evidence begun, for some reason, the Attorney General, dropped the whole suit.

Against one side of the New Grounds, next to the river, the Earl of Berkeley built a vast wall of large stones. These were very firmly crammed together, and the object was to break the violence of the waves from the river during a high tide, floods, or when the wind was in the wrong direction. This work at the time was known as the Hock Crib. It is held that in 1703 the tide was very high and faced a powerful wind. The whole area flooded to a depth of eight feet above normal.

The manor descended down through the Berkeley sons, until it came to a daughter called Elizabeth – the only child of Thomas Lord Berkeley. Richard Beauchamp, married Elizabeth and became possessor of the manor. He was rather unlucky in his children, because he only had three daughters, although they all married very well. Eventually the manor came into the ownership of George Nevil, Lord Latimer.

William, Lord Berkeley was created, the Earl of Nottingham and Earl Marshal, and he levied a fine on this manor to the use of King Henry VII, and his heirs male so all the estate eventually reverted to the Crown until the death of King Edward VI. After this, they went back to Henry, Lord Berkeley, the fifth in lineal descent.

The church of St John is largely perpendicular and is considered the same is early English from the fourteenth century, while the vault is thirteenth century. It is a rare and good example of English church building.

One old record states there was a parsonage, which was mooted a very rare occurrence in those days. This building has of course, long disappeared.

Another titbit of information concerns a family called Knight. Their very peculiar claim to fame is that for many generations, descendants were born with five fingers and a thumb on each hand. This is thought-provoking, because it is well-known that Queen Anne Boleyn, the second-fated wife of Henry VIII, also had five fingers, and a thumb. Later on in her short life this peculiarity became known as a mark of the devil.

At one time there was considerable trouble with the village called Awre on the other side of the river. On the Slimbridge side there was a piece of land also called Wharfe. The River Severn has always been notorious for changing its course, sometimes even overnight. At one time, the Wharfe ended up at the Awre, and the residents and villagers, the other side of the river, were quite delighted to acquire extra rich land. This did not last long, though, because with its next fit of temper the river reverted to its normal channel.

Gradually down the decades, Slimbridge became a kind of backwater until one great man arrived. He was the late Sir Peter Scott, son of Scott of the Antarctic. He was fascinated by the low-lying land, the wet marshes, and the river in general. He saw the immediate potential of what could be done for everyone's benefit by turning this large plot of land into a bird conservation area. And so was born the Slimbridge wetlands and wildfowl trust, famous throughout the United Kingdom.

Over the years, Sir Peter and his wife developed this area of land and today we have the most magnificent conservation and wildfowl trust. There are many walks for the dedicated birdwatchers to follow and hides at the appropriate places. There are the modern and necessary facilities for today's visitors with a shop, exhibitions, demonstrations and adequate parking for the great god motorcar. The whole is now known as the Wildfowl and Wetlands Trust.

For those who are more energetic and athletic, the lanes around this area are numerous and flat, quite perfect for walking and cycling. It is easy to reach from the motorway, or the main A38 road. Sir Peter must have been delighted at how what he started grew into an enormous, famous place for education and entertainment.

Stinchcombe

Stinchcombe is a parish in the Berkeley Hundred not a great distance from Dursley and only fifteen miles south of Gloucester. It is only small and for centuries was well-known for having superb arable land with fine pastures. It was also quite famous for both cheese and cider-making so was always well-known and relatively popular even though, at times, sparsely inhabited.

It is most uncertain what its early name really was. One record states it was Stears. Others though insist there were eight old names among which are Styntescumb and Stenescombe. It is agreed though that the translation of these mean a valley which was frequented by the sandpiper and the dunlin.

Wulfheah held it prior to the Conquest at one hide and no tax. There was one villager and one smallholder and this was held to be the actual land of William who was the son of Baderon of the Westbury Hundred.

The village was sited on the side of a lofty hill, which gave it first-class protection against even the wildest weather. At the top of the hill there is a large plain and, years ago, this was used extensively for football as is confirmed by the great historian Rudder. The west side of the hill commands the scenery below as far as Berkeley Castle. Sometimes, on a very good day, there are views into Somerset, the old Monmouth, Herefordshire, Worcestershire and even some parts of Wales.

At one time it was held that thirteen counties and thirty parish churches could be seen but the visibility on those days must have been quite exceptional. Perhaps the most dominant feature of this remarkable landscape is that of the River Severn with its many windings. This makes the scene's perfect foreground while, behind the water, there is the Forest of Dean and, beyond that, to one side, the lovely Welsh mountains.

It has always been known for the considerable variety of fossils which have often been found; an amazing variety of petrified cockles, muscles, scallops and other bivalves. This really displays to us that these hills are relatively young in the earth's age. Once the whole area was buried deep beneath some ancient sea and it is not all that difficult to visualise the traumas of volcanic eruptions and Ice Age convulsions. Man did not, could not, then exist and exactly when he did come upon the scene has not been proved satisfactorily.

In 1881 evidence was found though with the discovery of a flint weapon. It was a very fine stone axe discovered on Stinchcombe Hill. It was calculated that it had originally been made much larger and then was broken. It was utilised again by being chipped to fit into a handle. It was found in the angular gravel of the Cotswold Hills and gradual decomposition by various atmospheric influences among the oolitic rocks brought it to light. It was agreed the tool could only have been used by local inhabitants though the date given is simply and vaguely prehistoric.

When the Romans arrived they certainly found the Old British living everywhere even if in small tribal groups. Publius Ostorius Scapula did not like the British and he most certainly never trusted them. He set to and built a string of strong forts from Old Sodbury right up to Glevum, today's Gloucester. He built a fairly powerful fort known as the Drakestone Camp on Stinchcombe Hill from which he would just about have total dominance over the Britons plus excellent communications with Glevum in one direction and the large fort at Old Sodbury in the other.

There is not a lot of interesting information either before or after the conquest until we come to one outstanding man. He was a Tyndale, a family which had always had long connections with Stinchcombe. His name was William and he was born somewhere between 1494 and 1495. Some historians hold his birth was at Nibley; others plump for Stinchcombe, which was the family home. The confusion is made more complicated because there was an old tradition for the family to use other names and William sometimes used that of Huchyns. Not much is known about his immediate family except that his brother Edward became the general receiver for land in Gloucestershire and Somerset which belonged to Maurice, Lord Berkeley.

Tyndale went up to Oxford in 1510 and obtained his BA in 1512. Both of the great universities had now started to become influenced by a new spirit of learning. We do know that Tyndale spent some time as tutor to the children of Sir John Walsh of Old Sodbury but exactly when he developed his radical ideas is not certain, though grow they did.

He became utterly disgusted with the church and decided to translate the Bible, especially the New Testament, into the vernacular. He argued that even if the low people were illiterate they did have the right to hear their Bible spoken in their language. Very brave words for those times.

It was not all that long afterwards that he sailed for Hamburg where he met Luther. His whole life, to the point of obsession, became the task of translating the Bible. He and his copying secretary led precarious lives but gradually some copies of his Bible were smuggled into England. He was a very brave man and even stood up to denounce King Henry VIII's divorce, which was living dangerously because this King could be a dangerous enemy. It all had to end though and in only one way. He was caught, imprisoned and, despite gallant attempts by many friends, sentenced to be executed for heresy. He was strangled at the stake at Vilvords on the 6th October 1536 and his body burned.

He was an incredible man, a brilliant scholar. He had always lived in poverty with death at his shoulder and yet all knew him. What the Stinchcombe Tyndales thought is not really known.

There was another highly unusual character who has been long forgotten. In April 1791 there died at Dursley a Mr Bendal when aged seventy-six years. His claim to fame is weird. In 1731 he rode 1,000 miles in 1,000 hours on the same horse around Stinchcombe Hill. Why? We have no idea but it is most likely there was some heavy kind of bet involved because it was hardly a normal kind of exercise even for an eccentric.

There have been numerous aristocrats holding the manor from a William de Alba Mara down through the Braddeston family whose Thomas was advanced to become a peer of the realm. For many decades the Tyndales were considered the oldest and most respectable family. One though does appear to have become more than a little involved in politics in the reign of Charles I. He was very much alarmed at the approach of some Royalists and bolted to hide himself for three days and nights in a large yew tree. From this position he was aghast to see the Pinfolds' house, and his own, burned to the ground. So it is fairly obvious where his political beliefs lay.

Then little Stinchcombe relaxed back to its rural tranquillity. Only one other great event took place, which was in 1866. A memorial cenotaph was erected to William Tyndale, and this was inaugurated by the Earl of Ducie. It holds a dominant and prominent position with a cenotaph that can be seen for miles around. It is a steep scramble up the hill but worth every sweaty step to stand at the top and pay tribute to a hero, scholar and martyr, and to Stinchcombe itself.

Stow on the Wold

Stow on the Wold where the wind blows cold is the chant from some local wags and they are not far wrong either. Stow is at an elevation of 800 feet and there is precious little shelter when the winter gales blast forth. The temperature can be many degrees lower than anywhere else.

Today a few other jokers refer to Stow as 'Asleep-in-the-deep' and although it has never bristled with history, like so many other villages or little towns, it has always had a little something about it.

Records show it had seventeen old names which range from Eduuardestou, Stova down through to Stowe le Olde then Stowe in ye wolde. It is thought the actual word of Stow means a place where people gathered to worship.

It lies in the old Hundred of Slaughter and was once part of the great Maugersbury Estate. Indeed the Saxons referred to the little place by the name of Maugeresbury because in their language stow meant simply 'a dwelling'.

Stow's true age is a matter for considerable conjecture because there is a lot we do not yet know about the town. It is fairly certain that ancient Britons liked the region even if it was windy. They were practical people and, from this elevation, it was impossible for an enemy to swoop on them. Defence was relatively easy.

It is considered that Maugeresbury was their main place and it is even possible that Stow itself did not exist then. This opinion from some historians is still unproven but they may be correct. The primitive homes of the ancient Britons would not have persuaded them to live in such an exposed place as that of Stow. Perhaps they just had sentinels there, changing them on a rota basis.

It did though have another name and this is confirmed by Rudder in his great book of Gloucestershire. It was Edwardestowe and has been written like this in many ancient deeds. For many years, the locals referred to it as Stow St Edwards.

King Athelred gave one hide of land here to the church of St Edward which explains one name. Certainly by the time of Domesday in 1086, the name Stow was barely considered. It was simply a district of Maugeresbury, as old records insist. Yet strangely enough this latter town is shown as being in the Hundred of Salemones. All very confusing indeed.

We know it had twelve villeins, only one freeman and a priest plus six slaves which is rather a limited population even for those days. Why so small a number of people should warrant their own priest is simply another unanswered part of the puzzle.

The Abbey of Evesham purchased a charter of free warren in both of these small places in the reign of Henry III. And although both were small, Stow had the grant of markets and fairs, which hints there must have been some population growth by then. Markets and fairs were extremely important when travel was so difficult and virtually impossible for the villein class. Some historians consider that this was the time when Stow started to become the more dominant place.

Some evidence has been found of Neolithic remains in the shapes of axes but these were at Maugeresbury then known as Maethelgar's Burh. An earthwork, very much pre-Roman, was later found but that is all we know about this period until fresh discoveries are made.

The important family was that of John, Count of Tankerville. He came over to England with William I at the Conquest and, like so many others, his object was to feather his personal, family nest. He would have been loyal to his Duke but pragmatic enough to want reward for putting life and limb at risk. It is reasonably certain that he returned to Normandy but why we do not know.

He established a family and they stayed in England to become one of consequence. One was Lord Chamberlain to Henry I. Another held this position for King Stephen during the bloody fights between him and Matilda for the crown. Somewhere around this period it is felt the family name was changed to that of Chamberlayne.

All of these nobles married rather well and it would not be for anything so mundane as love. Marriages were made for political and economic alliances as well as rich dowries. These were the vital criteria in those cut-throat days of noble warrior politics. The feelings of young couples were of no consequence whatsoever.

Sir John Chamberlayne was a very great soldier and most prominent in the court of Edward III. A record in London says that the King granted to him, in the name of Count Chamberlayne, Earl of Tankerville, a warrant to receive 10,000 marks, which was an astounding sum then. This was for money which had been lent to the King's son in the French wars.

We know that in the thirteenth century, Stow's size was greater than it had been for generations. A century before, Richard de Clifford had a number of places razed to the ground with a view to modern expansion.

Towards the middle of that century we are positive about Stow's growth because it had twenty-seven tax payers. From 1357 onwards, Stow had become of sufficient importance to need a regular tax collector for the County though in 1381, only 166 people were actually assessed for the dreaded Poll Tax. Perhaps people even then had learned how to become adroit with their incomes when the word tax was mentioned.

Stow then entered a boom period. Because of its hilly elevation, it had always been perfect land for rearing sheep. Indeed, at a much later date, Daniel Defoe travelled around the countryside and he is known to have commented upon the vast numbers of sheep at Stow Market.

The markets and fairs were great affairs and very much red-letter days for everyone, especially the humble people. Stow itself would be crammed with horses, cattle, sheep and all of the goods associated with an agrarian life. At one stage it was considered the busiest place in the whole of Gloucestershire.

During the Civil Wars it also acquired a little burst of pure fame. This savage war often divided families; fathers and sons, brother against brother, and all over religion, basically. The two sides had absolutely nothing in common and each was violent in considering its cause was the only true one.

This lovely Cotswold countryside, with its gorgeous green-clad hills and superb old Roman roads, became the scene of a great battle in 1646. It was famed to be the last of these wars.

Sir Jacob Astley, already well into life's span, marched with over 3,000 men towards Oxford on the King's side. Unfortunately for him, he met Cromwell's superbly trained and highly disciplined army; an army where men held their positions on merit and not by rank of birth, wealth or right.

The Parliamentarians simply overwhelmed Sir Jacob and his men. They had no chance whatsoever. Sir Jacob himself survived but only 1,000 of his men. These were taken prisoner and locked in Stow's church, which must have made a considerable squeeze, to put it mildly.

Although defeated with a vengeance, Sir Jacob still had spirit. He uttered the famous, long-remembered words, "You have done your work well. Now you may go and play – unless you fall out among yourselves!"

There was no chance of that just because of Cromwell's discipline. Any of his men found brawling, fighting or even swearing were dealt with very harshly.

When it was all over with a new Charles II back on the throne in 1660, everybody's politics gradually simmered down once more though there were still odd rumbles from here and there.

Stow turned itself back to the more important business of making money and delving into commerce. The little town did indeed become quite affluent but what goes up must always come down.

There was another growth spurt in the seventeenth century when the lord of the manor and the burgesses had a thundering row over control of the town. That too was gradually resolved.

By 1675, Stow was described as a large but rather poor town, quite a turn-up for the book. A century later another traveller described it as indifferent to look at. In other words, it had enjoyed its brief flash of fame or notoriety, depending upon a person's political opinion. Now it was well past its prime, ready to sink into tranquil and rustic obscurity once more.

Today it is a quiet little place. Probably townies from elsewhere who scoot through in their cars on the Fosse rarely give it a thought. Neither does it enter many heads that their rubber wheels and smelly exhausts are connecting with the Fosse, built by the Romans nearly 2,000 years ago. Stow probably does not

care a hoot. After all, *it* knows it was once wealthy and famous
and enjoyed a little episode in this country's history. If people laugh
at its dead and alive aspect it is quite possible the people of Stow
grin to themselves then walk away muttering, "Sour grapes!"

Stroud

It appears Stroud only had six old names and three of these,
Strode, Stroode and La Stroud show there has been very little
change over the many centuries. In Saxon times it was called
Strogd which, when translated, meant many scattered houses,
all dispersed at some distance from each other. However, another
source hotly disputes this and insists the name means nothing
more or less than marshy land that was overgrown with
brushwood.

It is considered the first houses were built on the banks of
the River Froom which name adds to the general confusion
because there are three rivers with that name. There is another
in the next county and also one down at Yate. This name is
held to mean rapid, and Stroud's river, which rises near to
Brimpsfield, can hurry and bustle on its way at times. Some people
say it was the Romans who first used the name of Froma but
there is little proof.

It was part of the Bisley Hundred, though ignored by the clerks
who compiled the Domesday Book, which tells us it was obviously
just too tiny and inconsequential to warrant an entry in the great
book.

Ancient history is much more certain because it was all sea
which has been repeatedly confirmed by the many deposits and
fossils which have been found. This would probably be about
150 million years ago. At that time, today's valleys would not
have existed because they needed an Ice Age to make their form
and shape.

There are certainly many old burial grounds in the immediate locality which go back to the Neolithic and Bronze Ages and these are strewn around at Avening, Amberley, Cranhma, Uley, Selsey and Minchinhampton – the most well-known of which is considered to be that known as Hetty Peglar's Tump at Uley.

There were a number of local fortresses at Painswick and Haresfield as well as Uley. It was these old hill camps which were taken over by the Romans. Once they had established their dominant control over this region, they then turned their hands to building their lovely, centrally heated villas, the most notable and famous of which is that known as the Woodchester Pavement. This huge mosaic pavement covers forty-eight square feet and is situated in the old churchyard. It was the floor of the provincial governor's villa and depicts Orpheus surrounded by circles of birds and animals. It is exquisite but usually only uncovered every ten years for reasons of preservation. It is dated as built in the fourth century.

Rudder, the great historian, holds that the name of Stroud and Strand were one and the same, which is not as improbable as might first seem. Many people were in the habit of calling the banks of the river strands as they also separate various parishes.

Stroud always had lots of water from many rivulets, as well as the Froom, and it is these which are held to form many boundary lines. Above there is a lot of high ground while below is excellent pastureland with good soil. There are many beech trees though not so many as centuries ago, before husbandmen started to destroy them.

It was this excellent water that attracted weavers. A great many skilled Flemish weavers came over in the 1530s. In 1535 there was an Act which compelled all of the clothiers to weave their marks into each length of the cloth they made. Elizabeth I encouraged the Huguenots, who were fleeing from religious persecution, to enter the country. Many of these people were highly skilled at cloth-making and it was they who introduced the lighter-weight cloths that became so popular for the export trade.

The scarlets ands blues seen all over the area were those in huge demand for military uniforms but it is the former colour which is perhaps the more famous. These lengths of cloths could be seen drying in the fields, many raised on Tenters. Sometimes these were called tenterhooks from which has arisen the saying of 'being on tenterhooks'. The bright scarlets were particularly eye-catching with the blues as the contrast. In between, were the white houses so it was not long before the whole area shouted considerable prosperity.

Few of the clothiers actually lived in the town. At one stage it is known there were eighteen clothing mills with about thirty master clothiers according to the great historian Rudder. These were hard-bitten businessmen who preferred to be on hand where their cloth was made. Some of them became very rich men and as money is inclined to give power, they also became dogmatic. During this great boom period, the clothing industry gave work to many because it was all a tremendous occupation. The cloth provided constant work for the cottagers, from picking and cleaning the wool, to scribbling and spinning it. The yarn had to be spooled, warped, woven, buried, milled, rowed, sheared and drefted as well as being coloured for specific orders.

Spinning would often be sent by the clothiers as many as twenty miles or even more but it gave regular work to women and children who spent their short lives toiling in their humble and often very wet cottages. The income produced was enormous and it was not long before the clothiers put their heads together and decided water transport would be beneficial.

At one stage an application was made to Parliament to make the Froom navigable to the Severn and an Act was passed in 1730, but this never came to fruition. The next idea was that all loading should be in ships, two of which would ply between every couple of mills. At every mill there would be a crane to do all the very heavy loading. This scheme was tried but found to be rather unsatisfactory. The next idea was the canal, which would be forty-two feet wide and just for the movements of goods, especially the cargo of coal. Both the clothiers and the dyers used vast amounts of fuel for their work.

Then came trouble as some of the landowners formed an objection party to oppose any canal. They objected to giving up some of their land. The main idea was to run the canal from the Severn through Stroud and eventually make a connection with the River Thames. After much bitter wrangling, the clothiers won the day and the canal was laboriously constructed but not without other problems – the major one of which was the high Cotswolds. This required a long tunnel known as the Sapperton Tunnel and it was not bored without loss of life. There was no room for any towpath so the barges had to be 'walked' through. Two boards were laid amidships on which two men lay, with their heads inboard. The men's feet then 'walked' along the tunnel's wall to provide the barge's motive power. Even a strong man was in a state of exhaustion when the barge finally emerged into daylight again.

During the Civil Wars both the Cavaliers and the Roundheads often fought in the area. When Gloucester was under siege there were trenches on Painswick Beacon which were filled with Royalist troops. This was in the September of 1643. In the spring of that year there was a very violent battle roughly centred at Painswick because canon balls have been dug up at Stroud.

Even before this time, in 1395, the area was well-known to another famous person, Dick Whittington. Some sources say this was *the* Dick Whittington, later to be multiple Lord Mayor of London – he of the cat fame. It is agreed this family did hail from Pauntley and they held this manor for over a century. They did quite well for themselves because they also held Rodborough in the Minchinhampton Hundred, though one old record insists Rodborough was in the Hundred of Longtree.

Rodborough was the seat of the famous Sir Onesiphorus Paul, Baronet, also High Sheriff of the County. He was not the only famous person born there because in 1638 Richard Clutterbuck first saw some light of day. This sadly did not last long because by the age of twelve years he was quite blind.

This did not deter him at all. He walked up and down all the uneven ground around Rodborough without any guide. Nature compensated for his blindness by giving him the most incredible hearing. He could tell when an hourglass was running down with his ears, and he heard the lowest whisper in another room.

At the same time he showed an incredible ability as a mechanic. He made oatmeal mills, pepper mills and even the wheel for a cloth mill. He took a watch to pieces and mended it and made a splendid chain for his own watch. He made violins, bass viols and a set of virginals with double jacks. He also invented other improvements. He could also play each of his instruments. He taught music from a scale of his own forming and cut his notes upon a piece of wood. He ran a race of two hundred yards in length and was turned three times but this did not fox him at all. He was probably one of the most extraordinary men to come from, not just Rodborough, but the surrounding area of Stroud.

In May of 1755 Stroud also had another peculiar claim to notoriety. In the *Gentleman's Magazine* of the 19th August, there was a report of a loathsome plague of earwigs at Stroud. These insects did not just eat the flowers, fruits and garden produce, they invaded all the homes, being especially bad in wooden ones. Nothing and nowhere was sacred. The houses swarmed with earwigs. The cracks between timbers were filled with them. The floors were covered in moving masses. All the bedlinen in cupboards writhed and no food was safe. The records do not say from where these earwigs came nor how long this plague lasted so it can only be presumed they did not go until the cold weather set in.

Another snippet in an old record then talks about what took place in 1786 in the open square and the cross below Silver Street. A bull was tied up on a short rope, which was fastened to a heavy stone. The poor animal was then baited, though the record, probably trying to be charitable, says that great dogs were not set upon it. A final comment is made about this barbaric act in the hope it was the last time such would take place at Stroud.

Like so many other places in the County, the cloth industry began to slide into decline in the nineteenth century, from about 1830, but this was not all doom and gloom – although originally it may have seemed so to the cottage workers. The space which was left, plus the suddenly available labour force, gave the impetus to start up other trades, especially that of light engineering. Many of the old cloth mills underwent conversion into small factory units. Today there have been lots of new homes to satisfy the population.

This town, once minute and not worth a mention in Domesday, has come a long way since Neolithic man and its future seems assured. It is places like this that make the backbone of this country. Long may they remain in situ.

Tetbury

Tetbury had quite a few weird names to start with and these range from Tettan, Tectan and Tettan Bryg to name but a handful. Which came first is the old story of the chicken and egg.

One school of thought states all of the names indicate they mean Tette's fortified place or simply Burh to tell us it was an encampment. The feminine of the Old English personal noun of Tette might refer to the sister of the great King Ine, mother of St Guthlac, who was very active at Wimborne.

At the time of the Romans, the British tribe were the Dubonii who were quite outstanding people as they were cultured and minted their own coins. After them came the Hwicce who were forced to pay tribute to the more dominant Mercians.

This area was always well settled because the soil was good

for agriculture. More to the point, the higher parts of the land made excellent defensive positions against marauders. The Romans, always with a martial eye to the general lie of the land, promptly followed suit in using the land for defence.

The Old British called the place Caer Bladon though centuries later the Saxons, perhaps to be awkwardly different, used Tettebery. Caer originally meant a wall or enclosure. Rudder thinks these facts may have come from the ancient historian Geoffrey of Monmouth. Unfortunately, his works have not always been translated too accurately so much is still conjecture.

In the south east there was an ancient, strong camp. Tradition even calls this a castle. What we think of today as a castle is certainly not that which would have been erected then. This castle would have been built of timber which has long since rotted away. Other early records hint that a Donwall Malmutius, a king of some kind, also built himself a castle over 2,000 years ago. Again this poses a problem as this is both a Latin and thus Roman name and makes another insoluble mystery.

What is fact is that in 681AD a Saxon charter was drawn up concerning the grant of land for a monastic foundation. Who did this? Some records state it was King Aethelred. Others hotly dispute this and say it came from the Abbess Tetta and it is through her that Tetbury has its present name; all highly debatable and likewise improvable.

What is certain is that monks were in the region and they had problems of their own, certainly enough to cause a distraction to their religious life. The first of these was caused by water – or the lack of it. They were forced to move from the Grange to get a better water supply. Then snag number two reared its ugly head because now they lacked wood for their cooking fires. So once more, bag and baggage, they had to pack up shop and move elsewhere.

By the time of Domesday in 1086 Tetbury, although small to our eyes today, was considered a place of worth. The Domesday clerks recorded it had thirty-two villagers, two smallholders, two riding men and a priest plus nineteen slaves as well as a mill. The number of slaves is interesting because the greater their numbers to do all the donkey work then the larger and more affluent the area. Even Little Upton only a short distance away qualified for two slaves in its own right.

The mill is a bit of a puzzle because from where did it obtain its water? This was vital for motive power and Tetbury has never exactly been awash with this as later records prove.

During the Middle Ages, the Abbots of Gloucester, Evesham and Worcester all owned manors in the Cotswolds. In the fourteenth and fifteenth centuries, they jumped a later firing gun by starting to enclose with stone walls – still very much a feature of the region.

This was particularly harsh for the yeoman farmers who had no redress against such powerful men. They were thrown off their lands and farms that may have been in families for generations. So much for Christian charity.

During the later Middle Ages, wealth came to Tetbury with a rush. It grew as the centre of the wool stapling; buying wool and making it into cloth. It lacked all mills itself simply because of the ever present water difficulties.

By the end of the sixteenth century, Tetbury had the most enormous market and was one of the largest in the country. Wool was brought from as far away as Leicester and Kent.

The merchants and traders, suddenly flush with lots of money – more than they knew what to do with –went on a house-building spree. The stone that they used was a local one with a delightful, golden ochre colour. The nearby dependent towns of Painswick, Nailsworth and Chipping Camden did their own thing by going in for perpendicular churches.

The Chipping was a spacious area and it was here that two fairs were held annually on Ash Wednesday and the 22nd July. It took its name from Sax Leapan, to buy, because it was the place where objects were bought and sold.

Around this time, unusually, some people managed to live

to a ripe old age, quite rare for those disease-ridden days. Most extraordinary of all was one called Henry West who lived at Upton during the reign of James I. It is alleged he lived to the mind-boggling age of 152 years but it is thought most likely this was wishful thinking on the part of his descendants. It is alleged he had five wives. There were no children from the first four so he went rather over the top with number five and had ten children with her, which led to 100 grandchildren. Even the Guinness Book of Records could not swallow this one!

Tetbury was always plagued with water problems because of its elevation. The inhabitants had to buy their water at sixpence and sometimes even tenpence a hogshead. Quite a sum in those days. This went on until 1749 when a well was finally sunk, sited in the market place. It went to a depth of 104 feet. After this, other wells were sunk.

There is an odd twist to this tale. Many centuries later, a quarry was sunk for a turnpike road. A discovery was made which became the talk of the town. The labourers struck an ancient aqueduct which was thought to lead from the Whorwell Springs for some religious house.

Rudder informs us that at the time of the great book's writing, a farmer in the region undertook a dig and many incredible artefacts were uncovered. These included arrowheads, javelins, ancient horseshoes as well as spurs without rowells. Under an agger, coins came to light from the Romans, the Old English and the reigns of Edward the confessor, Stephen and Henry III.

Cobbett rode through the area on his famous ride and, though usually the dreaded scourge of all landowners, he was pleased at what he found. The wealthy were trying to look after the poor which, coming from such a forthright man, was a positive accolade.

With the industrial revolution, Tetbury's growth halted abruptly because the town was simply bypassed. There was not enough water available to drive mills' machinery. Also, in the north, there were great steam-powered mills and all the sweated labour mill owners needed. All of this helped to kill off the Cotswold woollen trade.

Only a short distance from Tetbury is today's tiny hamlet of Doughton. One of its early names was Aet Ductune in 885, the Ductun in 1236, Duchtune, Dogthorne and finally Dufton in 1641. It is thought this name means the Duck Farmstead.

There is a barrow there because in 1016 a great battle was fought between the English and the Danes. The latter came off the worse and were routed.

There is no mention of Doughton in Domesday, not even under Tetbury, so it must have been quite insignificant though the battle left one field known locally as Danes' End. Rather appropriate too.

The main owners of the estate were the Talboys and Clark families. Somewhere Talboys had a large house built though whether this was before or after he became the High Sheriff is not known. Neither is it at all clear where this house was sited which brings us to another interesting point.

In 1796 a landowner, descended from a Huguenot family, also made up his mind to have a fine house. He and his family had prospered in the wool trade so this seemed an eminently sensible action but it needed marriage to a rich heiress for building activity to commence.

Highgrove was finished in 1798 and as it stood 500 feet above sea level it had stunning views of Tetbury church. It ended up as a fine gentleman's residence. Early prints depict a house, which might, depending upon one's architectural taste, be admired. It stood four-square to the strong winds though some people might have uncharitably called it nothing but a stone box dumped down on a grazed field. It is thought the local man Keck may have been the architect.

In 1893 the house was nearly completely destroyed by fire, so hastily sold. It then passed through a queue of owners, most of the men in the military line. After World War II it was owned by Lt Colonel Francis Mitchell though only his mother lived at Highgrove.

The penultimate owner was Maurice Macmillan who died before his father, the Earl of Stockton, better known perhaps as a Conservative Prime Minister. Then it was on the market again and was purchased by His Royal Highness, the Prince of Wales as a private, country residence.

Today it is a thriving home and business devoted to organic farming. Once the Prince was scoffed at for these ideas of his but not any more. He was just a little ahead of the times. He gardens and farms organically with tremendous results, which benefit not only his business ventures but also the wild life.

Prince Charles has made a resounding success of Highgrove's land and now all is greatly admired. He has even improved the harsh outlines of the original house with an attractive palisade on the roof coupled with urns.

As a king was reputed to be in the area 2,000 years ago, it seems appropriate to have the heir to the throne in the region once more.

Tetbury itself is now a highly attractive little town. There is the old-world marketplace for the visitors; a police museum which is unusual and a brisk air of tranquillity but also sober business. It is an England which has not been ruined or spoiled and it bristles with our history.

The Three Sodburys

There have always been three distinct Sodburys; Chipping, Old and Little. Some records consider that for many decades Old Sodbury was that which was dominant. All of this region was the tribal territory of the Dubonii tribe, long before the Romans invaded.

When the Romans did finally reach this part of the island

they appreciated the superb hill-top position from the rim of the escarpment. It did not take them long to find the old camp which some records think may have been from the Iron Age. The Romans were not at all bothered by historical niceties. What appealed to them was the actual site because, being very practical people, they immediately saw the possibilities and promptly established their own fort. From here they were able to keep the Dubonii under their thumbs.

It is reasonable to assume the two races rubbed uneasy shoulders although there would obviously be those among the Britons who would ape or toady everything Rome to feather their own nests. Derisively called tame Britons.

Each of these Sodburys had a variety of old names from which have descended our present ones. Chipping Sodbury had sixteen with a variety of spellings, three of which are Sophire, Sodbury Mercata and Chepyng Sudbury.

Old records give some interesting facts about some of the street names. Today's Horse Street was precisely where horses were sold. Rounceval Street was once known as Runeualestrete or Romsefalle. This appears to translate to fat, boisterous and loose women.

A long vanished street was that of Mortstreyte, probably from the word morte which meant harlot. This raises the interesting question as to what shenanigans took place in the little town for streets to be named after harlots and fat, boisterous, loose women!

Another long-vanished street was that of Shoutinge Lane where the tenements also included Brown's Shambles. Nearby was the Sceamol, which meant a stall from which meat was sold in the open. A further record insists there was also shop 'voc' le Stithes which, in 1574, caused argument when it was said the last word should read Smithes. It seems to be connected with a forge though this would not necessarily mean a blacksmiths or farriers. It could refer to a garret or simple attic.

Little Sodbury had only thirteen old names, among which are Sopeberier and Parua Schobia.

Old Sodbury holds the record with twenty-five old names and spellings, two of which are Soppanbyrig and Sobyr. It is agreed these all mean Soppa's fortified place, but who was he? We have no idea.

All of these places were in the Hundred of Grumbald's Ash, which covered an extensive area. Before William I, this was all owned by the Saxon Brictric, a man who made a real mess of his life because of an inability to understand the workings of the female mind. The Norman Lady Matilda fancied Brictric very much. What he really thought of her we have no idea. Maybe he was simply flattered or arrogant enough to play fast and loose with Matilda's feelings. Whichever it might have been, he suddenly ditched Matilda.

If she had been the one to make the running, it is easy to understand her humiliation and fury. This rejection certainly rankled deeply as Matilda cast her eyes over the eligible males for her rank. She finally settled upon the most powerful of them all, William I.

As soon as William had taken England, Matilda acted. She had Brictric seized and thrown into prison while she took all of his lands for herself, obviously aided and abetted by her powerful husband. Now we come to two stories, neither of which can be proved. The first says that Brictric died in prison, while the second insists he outlived Matilda, was released at her death but left quite landless. In those days this meant just about destitute.

Domesday tells us that Old Sodbury, at the time of King Edward, consisted of ten hides, a park and eighteen servi or slaves, which reinforces the ancient dominance theory. It is reasonable to state these figures covered the three Sodburys because it was most unlikely the Domesday clerks would bother to split such figures into three when the places were so close together.

Little Sodbury has an ancient manor house that was once the seat of the Stephen's family, a very old family in the region. In 1521, it had a visitor who enjoyed the lavish hospitality normal for those times. He was William Tyndale who lived with Sir John Walsh to tutor his children.

There is a weird story about when these children became adult. They were at dinner in 1556 when there was the most dreadful thunderstorm. The lightning burst through a window and killed one of the youngsters present and the father was so badly injured that he too died a few weeks later.

During Tyndale's stay with the Walsh family he started to be heavily persecuted. It was probably his own fault because he knew the area swarmed with bigoted priests but Tyndale was never afraid to put his money where his mouth was. He despised all priests and with good reason. He resented deeply the rigid hold they held over the ordinary people who were mostly illiterate. He was scornful at their corruption and did not hesitate to say so. He was so outspoken that Lady Walsh was forced to rebuke him personally.

Tyndale acted promptly by translating a small book written by Erasmus which railed against the wrongs of the monks and friars. He gave this to Lady Walsh who was infuriated with him. To give her due credit she did read the book and realised Tyndale was correct with his views.

Tyndale then announced, while with this family, he would translate the Bible's New Testament into English, a language that could be understood by the ordinary man. He made his famous vow and statement, "If God spares my life, I will see the day that a boy who drives the plough will know more about the Scriptures than the priests!" After that, of course, he had to leave the area and then the country. He went to Europe to do this great work but ended up being strangled at the stake, then burned.

The manor is still there as a private residence. To one side, almost facing the drive, is a steep uphill path. When climbed this brings a person on to the high land where it is quite easy to work out the dimensions and general layout of the old Roman fort.

Old Sodbury has always been hilly and with stunning views

of fine, rolling pasture land with the town of Yate easily discernible. On especially fine days, the higher land of Wales can be seen. Not far away there is a round tower but this is not an ancient monument. It is a ventilation shaft to the railway deep below.

It is held that Chipping was added to the name after the market was established during the reign of Henry III. It is a market town though initially this market was not too popular with the people for some odd reason. It is dairy country, which means plenty of cheese to sell, but gradually this changed.

Chipping Sodbury has a good town plan that was drawn up by William Crassus in the twelfth century. It had Borough status until 1681 with the civic head the bailiff. Then Charles II gave the town a spanking new Charter of Incorporation which placed complete jurisdiction under a mayor, six aldermen and twelve burgesses. Seven years later, for some unknown reason, the townsfolk agitated to return to the original set up. They wanted their bailiff back with ten burgesses, so this was restored. The people of this town were obviously an independent-minded bunch who called a spade just that. Much later when the public lavatories were constructed they bluntly said *MEN* and *WOMEN*. Usually the words would have been *GENTLEMEN* and *LADIES*.

There is an interesting little story about the old-fashioned word of burling from Gloucestershire Notes and Queries. It concerned the death of Mrs Hathway who was supposed to have poisoned her husband. A witness stated that Mr Hathway invited him into the pub for a beer or to 'have a tip'. The witness declined. But Mr Hathway went in for a quart of beer, came out again, then the witness entered. He was told to 'burl out the beer as he was in a hurry'. It appears this is a good old Anglo-Saxon word which translates to 'carouse' or pour out liquor. What happened next we don't know because the records go tantalisingly quiet.

The church here was the scene for one marriage which would produce an unusual and fated offspring. It was that of the parents of Thomas Chatteton on the 25th April, 1749. Their son was a remarkable poet but his work was not appreciated while alive. He tried to pass off his writings as newly discovered ancient manuscripts and killed himself aged seventeen years.

Chipping Sodbury has changed very little down the centuries. It echoes antiquity and history, so much so that, a few years ago, a Czech visitor, completely fascinated, insisted upon hiking everywhere, leaving Wallis utterly exhausted.

Two old pumps still remain and beneath one there is the well, which goes down twenty-seven feet. There were more pumps once and the reason was sheer practicality. Animals at market have to be watered regularly.

It is considered the first cross was erected about 1350, though this was demolished later to be replaced with another in 1553. It has been a wandering cross, sitting at many sites, but it now holds its current position since 1920 as the war memorial.

Horse Street was once a turnpike road because there was a huge volume of traffic to and from Bristol. In this street there was also an apothecary whose assistant was to find world fame in saving mankind from the hideous disease of smallpox; Edward Jenner.

It is also possible to find another vital link with the past because there is a small plaque which told the fire brigades of old the house was insured and they would all get paid.

Tudor House is considered the oldest property and used to be owned by the Master Weavers. It is now the local headquarters of the Conservative Party but, in the past, has also been a doss house.

Probably the jewel in this crown is the Town Hall which is magnificent. Inside are relics of long ago which include the Town Seal, the mayor's chair and an enormous Town chest. This latter was carved from one single block of oak. It is strapped with great iron bands and its weight is .75 of a ton. It still has its keys which hang nearby, companions to the Town mace.

At the rear of the church there is a short but quite delightful walk by the banks of the little River Frome. Where this walk ends the visitor can turn into Brook Street, which, long ago, was the main road into the town. The bridge here is very old and known as the Medieval Bridge.

Although there are some modern houses, Chipping Sodbury has retained its history and with its broad street and very old buildings, it complements the other two Sodburys making all three a 'must' on the tourist trail.

The Noose

Just over four miles north from Sharpness, a part of the River Severn is called The Noose, which is an excellent descriptive name. The river goes into a huge bulge before making an abrupt turn to the west to narrow very sharply. It heads in this direction for a very short distance then turns sharply to the north before swinging back eastwards. This leaves a spit of land, surrounded on three sides by the river and on the fourth by the Stroud water canal. It is a very watery spot yet for centuries has had a sprinkling of little villages and hamlets.

There are three which may be called sitting on the spit of land, especially Arlingham and these have as neighbours four others. Fretherne and Saul have often been lumped as one place and Rudder, the great County historian, describes them as having 'most unwholesome air' and whose inhabitants constantly suffered from the Ague. With so much water on all sides it is not at all surprising the area was considered very unhealthy.

Fretherne had eight old names that range from Fridorne to Frythyngthorne, which translated to mean a thorn tree where sanctuary could be found.

Saul had only five old names from Salle to Sawe and these simple words meant nothing more than a simple willow clearing.

Arlingham did a little better with eight old names, which

included Herlingham and Erkingeham. These may mean a homestead or water meadows of Eorl's or Eorla's folk, whoever they were. It is thought these names were pure Scandinavian and from the Old Norse but this is most uncertain. The word of Eorl means a warrior or nobleman and might even refer to the Earls of Berkeley.

Frampton's nine old names just meant a farmstead near to the river and if any of this small gaggle of villages and hamlets could be said to be dominant over the other, perhaps it is Frampton on Severn. Certainly history did not lightly pass these little places by as of no consequence. They all faced constant hazards from the capricious flooding of the Severn yet the river was also of vital importance in other ways.

It provided first-class and swift communications, yet could also be an obstacle against the same. It provided important fish food and it must have given constant shocks with its often erratic course changes because only a fool could state with certainty the river's course from month to month.

It was considered to be in the Bibury Hundred though this region has always had boundary troubles, which would not be resolved until the nineteenth century. Some records argue the Hundred was that of Whitstone or even Blakelow. What is known is, prior to the Conquest, it was held by a thane of King Edward called Cynwy Chelle. Domesday says there were twelve villagers, one smallholder but also sixteen male and female slaves so the area did have popularity.

There was a passage across the Severn to Newnham and some historians are adamant that Fretherne is to be identified with Fethanleag where in 584 Ceawlin and his brother Cutha fought a battle against the Britons, which was to prove fatal to Cutha.

Frethern always claimed it had the right to toll free in all markets with free passage over the Severn, yet it is Frampton which captures the imagination. This is said to be the birthplace of the Fair Rosamund who became the mistress of King Henry II. She is thought to have been a member of the big Clifford family and later the mother of William Espee, Earl of Salisbury.

It is held she was born in the twelfth century, and her real name was supposed to be Jan Clifford and she only used the Fair Rosamund as her *nom de guerre*. She was held to be a very lively girl of great wit who adored wearing see-through clothes to tantalise the men.

The story goes that she was seduced by Henry II at a very early age with the connivance of her governess. This King had a huge reputation with all females so there must have been something very different to Rosamund because it is held that Henry fell hook, line and sinker.

Henry was very much his own man and did exactly as he pleased. He lived with Rosamund in open adultery and did not care a fig for public opinion, let alone that of his hapless Queen. It is rumoured there was a secret passage to Henry's house though this is questionable. Whatever his faults, Henry was a very open King because he just did not care what people thought about him – as long as they obeyed him.

There are a variety of unproven stories about Rosamund's death. One is that Henry's Queen quietly arranged for her to be poisoned. Another insists she left the King because his amorous behaviour was too much even for Rosamund. A third tale says she had no great love for him either as King or man and went to become a nun. He was certainly much older than her and perhaps she had become tired of him and had her eyes on a younger swain. We will never know.

If the next part of this saga is true it is macabre. It is that the King, riding poste haste, insisted upon Rosamund's coffin being opened so he could see her for the final time. Henry was a very tough man but what he saw sickened him and all of the other witnesses. She had turned a foul, dark colour which does lend credence to the poison story. It certainly grieved King Henry and might, perhaps, explain his later erratic actions with Thomas a' Beckett.

The whole low-lying area has always been subjected to violent floods, which were especially bad in 1483, again in 1606. There was a huge storm with a south west gale and many animals were drowned and homes ruined. The records then say the 'somer' following had a violent heat wave and a winter with some of the most fearsome frosts ever experienced. (See River Severn.)

In an old record of 1586 it says a curate had been heard making seditious speeches; about what though and why? In that time information was also received about a new outbreak of men from Gloucester robbing vessels laden with corn and salt. Before that though, in 1385, a priest was murdered at the instigation of one Richard Clifford of Frampton. He was found guilty but only received a paltry fine and yet again the records stay frustratingly silent.

There was another startling event in 1826 when the Reverend Burden of Stroud stated a whale had been seen swimming up river towards the Noose. "What is known is that in 1885, down at the small village of Littleton on Severn near to Thornbury, a whale was indeed beached. It was a female Fin whale, almost seventy feet long with an estimated weight of about fifty tons. It died on the little beach and its death bought instant fame to the village and the river in general.

"Therefore it is reasonable to suppose that when the River Severn was running very high, whales did indeed travel up it. The event of 1826 year has just a mere mention in the old records but some of these old stories are full of truth. When one considers the huge bend at the Noose plus the ferocity of the River Severn at all times, nothing is really surprising."

And what do we have today? Quiet little villages, nestling cheek by jowl, yet places of habitation still bounded by water on all four sides. The river's power has not abated. A visit there gives the distinct impression that life carries on but only with the mighty river's consent. Any time, any day or night, the Severn could easily throw another damaging fit of temper just to remind man how puny he really is.

The Tunnel

For countless generations the people of Gloucestershire and the old Monmouthshire had eyed the mighty River Severn and muttered about some kind of a tunnel. The river could be so dangerous to try and cross in any kind of vessel or ship and there was a constant need for better communications. A tunnel would be ideal.

In 1812 a general idea was mooted that a tunnel could be dug under the river and men enthusiastically started work. They were far too premature and lacking in engineering technology. They also found themselves defeated by an incredible phenomena. They had hastily to abandon the whole idea when their tunnel started to flood with water leaking in from below. There was a very powerful underground spring or stream and they simply could not cope.

Even right from the start in those early days, it was appreciated the problems would be enormous and the danger to workmen considerable. After the first fiasco, it still remained nothing but talk and wishes until the advent of the railways. Their arrival provided the necessary impetus. There simply had to be a tunnel, which the trains could use to cut journey times.

As always, the Severn's huge rising tides were of immediate concern, the second highest in the world. These are caused by the river's extra wide mouth and the complexities of the currents around the south of Ireland, Cornwall and South Wales. As the river's channel decreases so rapidly, backed up by these currents, a tide of fifty feet above the low water mark was quite common.

In 1871 detailed plans were presented to Parliament and in the next year, an Act was promulgated but before the work could start, provision had to be made for homes for the workmen.

On the Monmouthshire side, a shaft of fifteen feet in diameter was drilled to test the strata. This went to a depth of two hundred feet though progress was extremely slow. In four to five years only one shaft was sunk which became known as the Old Shaft though there was a drive of 1,600 yards heading towards the river.

So fresh contracts went out again and now a shaft was sunk on the Gloucestershire side at New Passage with headings to be driven both east and west. In 1877 a pumping station was erected with two Bull engines with a fifty-inch cylinder and a ten-foot stroke.

At the end of 1879 there were three additional shafts but the heading had still not advanced very far. Not a great amount of water had been met though the men were always acutely aware that the river's bed dipped sharply at a spot called The Shoots.

Then in October the men tapped into a huge body of water. This poured into the workings with such force that in twenty-four hours they were all full to the level of the river's tidal mark. Luckily the men had had warning and they managed to get out just in time to avoid loss of life.

So for seven years' labour there was very little to show, and this flooding nearly became the final straw. Mr A Walker took over under the chief engineer Sir John Hawkshaw at a time when spirits and morale were very low. The great engines stood idle; the boilers were out of steam and most of the workmen had left to find better and more reliable work elsewhere. At the same time, the water in the heading was very high.

Pumping out the heading was priority number one so two new pumps were obtained. One was a Cornish beam engine with a seventy-five-inch cylinder to work a plunger pump while the other was twenty-eight inches and would work two bucket pumps.

The contract was precise. The tunnel was to be 7,942 yards long, just over four and a half miles but the total length of the railway on each side would take this distance to seven miles and five furlongs. It also stated categorically that the dreaded Shoots must be dealt with first.

The cuttings at both ends of the tunnel were to have embankments several feet higher than the highest record tide.

The whole was to be lined with best bricks between two and three inches thick and their mortar could only be made from one part Portland cement mixed with two parts of clean, sharp silver sand.

It was still thought the chief danger would always be from The Shoots. No one had the foggiest idea that within a quarter of a mile lay real trouble.

A shield was made from oak to fit into the headings as tightly as possible and, when in position, heavy struts of timber would jam it into place. The great problem then arose of actually doing this. This equipment could only be lowered and fixed into place by divers. At that depth the pressure was great. More water had to be removed which, in turn, meant even more powerful pumps. For the tunnel to go under The Shoots, there had to be a gradient of at least one in a hundred. More and larger engine houses were erected on both sides but flooding came back when a pump broke through a defect. It took a huge effort to remove the broken pumping rods because there were also baulks of timber, each forty-five feet long.

Finally, in that October, work could start once more. In the panic from the spring flood, a vital door had been left open. Only a diver could shut it and this meant he would have to walk 1,000 yards up the heading. He would have to trail his air hose after him. He would have to go through the door on the 'wrong' side, shut a valve flap, come back to the 'right' side, pull up two rails of the tramway and then, and only then, close the offending door.

It was a mammoth, highly dangerous task, which must be done under the most appalling conditions. The strongest man alive simply could not pull 1,000 feet of hose behind him. The task and the walk would have to be made in the pitch dark, in deep very cold water and over debris and tools left behind in the spring flood panic.

Three divers were engaged. One would stand at the shaft bottom to pass the hose along. A mate would go up the heading for 500 feet to guide the air hose then the lone, incredibly brave third diver would have to go forward by himself.

Lambert, the diver in question, started out again and again in these foul, terrifying conditions. He was utterly defeated by the sheer magnitude of the task.

On the surface, the first very primitive oxygen cylinder was strapped to his back. With enormous courage he went back down again while the men on the surface chewed their nails and wondered whether they would ever see him again. They fretted about his safety and could do nothing to help him if anything went wrong. This time he did succeed. The whole exercise had been to make a vital repair on an eighteen-inch pump.

By December all the water had gone, then, in January 1881, Nature decided to take a hand in these proceedings. Without any warning whatsoever, there came a great snowstorm in which everything on the surface ground to a halt. This made a critical situation. Lack of coal meant the pumps would cease to operate and, once again, the water would get back into the headings. There were frantic efforts to get enough coal so the fires would stay alight, steam would be made and the pumps kept going.

Another crisis arose with the workmen. They often worked a ten-hour shift with a miserable thirty minutes for a meal. The men who pushed the skips, called runners, were nothing but two-legged labouring animals. These skips had to be pushed a great distance. What with one thing and another, antagonism rose to strike proportions. This did not last long though because men were too desperate for the work.

The explosive used was called tonite because it gave off less fumes underground than dynamite. At the Chepstow side, an arrangement had been made with Dr Lawrence for him to look after the sick and injured men. The majority of health problems though affected the lungs, caused by heat, damp and careless exposure when the men finished work.

On the 6th December 1882, the day shift suddenly emerged from the headings. They were bleeding, their clothing torn and they were frightened out of their wits crying that water had broken in once more. Hearts sank with dismay. Was it The Shoots at last?

Mr Walker and others hastily descended. In the dreadful gloom they met sheer chaos. Broken equipment, injured, deserted men, jumbles of clothing and tools – all abandoned in sheer animal panic – with just a trickle of water. It came from a flowing stream.

They ascended and there stood the sheepish and shame-faced day shift while the waiting night shift mocked them. They went down and soon put matters to right and the day shift had a lot of trouble living down their panic.

By 1883 more shafts had been sunk with even more pumps. In that year some more water did break in but it was clean and sweet-tasting and this was thought to come from an unsuspected natural reservoir. It took the pumps a little while but they coped and drained all this away again.

On the 17th October there was a great gale, which arrived with the high tide, all of which entered the local houses. Then the advancing waves reached the pumping houses and out went the vital fires. Finally, the water cascaded down into the tunnel.

There were eighty-three men trapped down there and they had to keep retreating but, even in the dark and under horrific conditions, they kept their heads. The tide turned just in time when the water was only eight feet from the ceiling and little boats could rescue the men. That was a night of unmitigated hell for all concerned.

Another new engine house was built with four more huge pumps. One million bricks were ordered per month so that, by the end of 1883, one mile of continuous tunnel at the Gloucestershire end was completed. In that year, 1,641 men were employed on the Gloucestershire side and 1,987 at the Monmouthshire end. Rails were laid and another pump, a monstrous affair, started to work, which meant there were always two pumps in reserve.

During the whole construction, enough water was pumped

out which would have formed a lake three miles square and ten yards deep but man had triumphed.

The first passenger train from London to South Wales passed through on the 1st July 1887 without a hitch and goods traffic began on the 1st September.

Since that remarkable engineering construction, trains have used the Severn Tunnel regularly and it is a credit to sound and brilliant Victorian engineering.

Thornbury

Thornbury is a little town with a large history sometimes very convoluted. Its ancient inhabitants go back for thousands of years because it is known that both Neolithic and Bronze age man carved himself a tiny settlement of crude huts.

How they called the area we do not know but later on Thornbury did acquire a variety of names. A few of these range from Turneberia, Tornberia, Thornebirlik and Torbyr and from just this handful it is simple to see from how we obtain today's name. A very rough and ready translation of all of these names means a 'fortified place' or one 'overgrown by thorns'. Take your pick.

Naturally, the Romans were also here in force because some of their coins have been found as well as shards of their pottery though no remains of any buildings yet.

The area passed to William II of Rufus notoriety. This King gave the whole lot to Fitzhamon for services which had been rendered, while the tiny church was donated to the Abbots of Tewkesbury because it was they who collected the tithes from Thornbury as well as appointing the vicar – right up to the time of the Dissolution and King Henry VIII.

We do know that in 1086, at the time of Domesday, there was a thriving market in the town, which even then had the potential to become a Borough. An extra impetus to development came between 1243 and 1262 when Richard of Clare, the Earl of Gloucester and Hereford, made an offer to people to settle in Thornbury. The offer was that those who were prepared to up-sticks would benefit from all the liberties and customs that were enjoyed by the burgesses of Tewkesbury. This was of considerable importance.

As manors went, Thornbury was rich and the shrewd Clares increased their control over this wealth with an extensive programme of imparking. In other words, land grabbing and fencing in.

With numerous marriages, the manor passed from crown control into those of the Clare family followed then by the Staffords and the Howards.

It is thought there may have been some kind of castle present in the twelfth century because, by the end of the next one, the Clares had their court in the town. It seems there might have been a mansion because by 1330 a great hall was certainly in use. Around this would be the residential and domestic offices for the numerous retainers so the town started to expand.

By the fourteenth century, the manor had passed to the Stafford family and there was an itinerant court as well as being the retinue of a powerful magnate.

Henry Stafford, Duke of Buckingham, fell out of favour for some reason and was executed in 1483 and his heir was only six years old. After Henry VII came to the throne, Buckingham's widow married Jasper Tudor who was an uncle to the King.

It was in 1498 that the boy heir attained his majority and took over his inheritance. Right from the start he showed he had grandiose ideas and, in 1510, as the third Duke of Buckingham, Constable of England, he applied for and received a licence from Henry VIII to build his own castle. His wish was to combine this with a college of great learning so he started off by snatching more land on an inparking exercise and was

176

loudly cursed by all and sundry. Henry's licence gave him another one thousand acres.

It is unfortunate that his magnificent plans for great learning did not apply to his own mind and tongue. The Duke had a choice between building on a huge scale or dabbling in the politics of the day. He also did not appear to appreciate he was born related to the crown and any wise sovereign always kept an eye upon such highly positioned men – just in case.

The Duke was also very proud and had ostentation, which can be twisted under matters political. In 1508 he decided to entertain upon a lavish scale. With his guests and their friends, 519 sat down for dinner with another 400 for supper. Once again we come upon two different stories as to what actually happened next. The first is that he spilled water over Cardinal Wolsey's shoes. The second, if that should happen to be the truth, was grave. It alleges he made the terrible error of a foolish jibe about Wolsey's father being nothing but a common butcher. How Wolsey must have seethed with humiliation.

What is known is that Wolsey at this time most certainly had the ear of King Henry VIII with a vengeance. Henry was a highly educated and very intelligent man. He was though also a very dubious friend and could, at the same time, be a vicious enemy as some of his wives were to find out. He had an elephantine memory for slurs and insults. He acted in wrath at this insult to Wolsey and by 1621 it was all over. Buckingham had been arrested, arraigned for treason and executed. His lands were confiscated by Henry who used the place as a royal demesne for thirty-three years. In 1535 he stayed there for ten days with Anne Boleyn. Later on Mary Tudor also lived there but when she became Queen, she returned the castle to the unfortunate Duke's heir.

As a pure castle, the building was unfinished although it had been crenellated. The son who finally took up this inheritance was desperately short of money so his father's ambitious schemes were never realised.

In 1811 Lord Henry Howard tried to do something about what

was becoming a local eyesore. He did restore the south tower and began to rebuild parts of the castle. Forty years later, the distinguished architect, Anthony Salvin, took over and, in 1854, the castle was finally finished but much more restrained than had been originally planned.

Today Thornbury Castle is an imposing structure and in 1982 it was opened as a private hotel, now famous for its luxurious apartments and general cuisine.

Rather like Tewkesbury, Thornbury was laid out in a 'y' shape. The long and very wide street was for markets for both cattle and cheese sales. It became quite famous as the place to go for good animals and food.

It is to the credit of Thornbury Town Council and Trust that the town retains so much of its old world charm yet, at the same time, still manages to provide modern housing.

There is an excellent tourist board and full details of fascinating walks may be obtained with a potted history because on the traveller's itinerary, Thornbury should not be missed.

Tortworth

The records show that Tortworth was in the Hundred of Grumbald's Ash, but what exactly is a Hundred? It is an old land measurement, intelligent and accurate, in use long before William and his conquest.

A Hundred comprised 100 hides. A hide was considered to be the amount of land capable of supporting one family and their animals. So obviously a Hundred, made up of 100 hides, was suitable for 100 families.

Another important point of the measurement was it indicated a Hundred was expected to produce 100 soldiers when needed, while the hide gave only one. These were very important sums long before the Conquest.

The actual word for hide derives from Higid or Higman which meant, quite simply, a household. In Old English, the word Hundred came from 'Hund' to mean 100 and 'red' told the reckoning. It was all quite simple and clear to all; certainly much clearer than some of today's rates' bills.

The origins of Tortworth's name descend from Torteworde, Tortary and Torhta. It is thought that these words mean an enclosure.

The unrecorded Old English of Torhta might well be a classic example of simple child's talk – just a pet name or diminutive from other names. We simply have no idea, though historians delight in arguing this point.

Domesday does not tell us much either. The hamlet must have been very small indeed, because all William's book says is that there were six villagers and seven smallholders, yet oddly enough, six slaves plus three mills.

The slaves make quite an imbalance for such a tiny population, so it can only be presumed they worked at the mills. What did these make, though? Cloth, or were they just corn-grinding? Even with Domesday, quite a lot is often left for speculation.

There was an ancient seat near to the church long before the Ducie family came upon the local scene. One early record in Rudder mentions Nicholas de Kyneston, called the lord of the manor.

It seems Nicholas went in for some dubious kind of horse-trading. He swapped some of this land elsewhere to get Tortworth though, infuriatingly, we have no idea of what attracted him. He did not stop there either. He purchased the rights to fairs and other privileges in the manor, so obviously Tortworth had something about it.

He only had a daughter as heiress and she had a most unusual name. This was Hawise. She became the widow of Robert de Veel and it was then the manor passed into that particular family. They were sometimes referred to as le Veel, all very confusing when looking back at old records. Sometime afterwards, the manor passed down to a male heir, at other times to the heiress.

One owner via matrimony was Sir David Matthews, who had five daughters. Such one-sex offspring certainly would occasion comment in those days when the male heir was the be-all and end-all of life. More to the point, it kept the precious family name going.

Then upon the scene came Sir Thomas Throckmorton, who married one of the six daughters and co-heiresses of Thomas Whittington of Pauntley. It is reasonable to consider this an offshoot of the family of the famous Dick Whittington, he of London and cat fame.

Sir Robert Ducie, baronet, alderman of London, came from the Staffordshire branch of the Ducie family and he bought Tortworth manor. He became the High Sheriff of Gloucestershire in the reign of Charles I. During the civil wars, though, he was taken prisoner by William Waller. He died unmarried, which was very rare indeed.

So it was his brother who inherited and also became the High Sheriff in 1660. This was an important year when Charles II returned from exile to claim his executed father's throne.

This brother was made a Knight of the Bath at the king's coronation, and then later created a viscount, so he did rather well for himself.

Whether there was some kind of jinx on the owners of Tortworth manor is uncertain, but this lord also died without an heir. It went down to a younger brother's daughter. There could not have been so many manors in those times that had such trouble in getting male heirs. Before the days of viagra, of course.

Strangely enough, there was another manor in the same parish which had exactly the same problem and worry. This belonged to Harry Wogan and when he died all he managed to leave was an heiress aged eleven. Was it perhaps the water?

There is little recorded about the mills, which is a pity. But as the whole county was involved in the cloth trade, we must guess that they were for this purpose.

Tortworth did have one outstanding claim to fame or notoriety. A tree, but what a tree! It is either an object of pure curiosity, or something Frankenstein would have adored.

It is very old for this country and Rudder talks little about it. It is a Spanish chestnut tree and Rudder simply says it had been there since 1216.

Across the hamlet's small paddock, there is a tiny spinney and the tree reigns in it. A huge part of this tree has died, yet there are still many branches which go into full leaf. In the eighteenth century it was measured and produced a girth of eighteen yards. On a dull day with drizzle falling, the tree is positively macabre and those with a vivid imagination should keep away.

It is a tiny hamlet today, no longer capable of being classed as a village and it appears to have changed little over the centuries. What did alter the landscape was a grand house.

Mr Leigh bought it from Lord Ducie and it was called Tortworth Court, listed Grade II. It was built between 1849 and 1852 and the architect was Teulon.

This house has also had its fame. There was a huge fire in 1991 from some unknown source and enormous damage was done. Now, though, it has been modernised after extensive rebuilding and is the Tortworth Court Four Pillars Hotel. Peels Leisure Club is in part of the house with everything the heart can desire. The £20 million refit has transformed this mansion into a 212-bedroom luxury hotel.

Of the estate itself, there have been great changes. Part is a remarkable arboretum with many magnificent trees, planted in the nineteenth century. A little stream trickles at the bottom of a fairly steep hill and follows a well sign-posted path through the arboretum.

During World War II, Tortworth Court became an American forces' hospital, then a prison officers' training school. Much of the area is now owned by the Home Office because of Leyhill Open Prison.

Permission to explore the arboretum is only given for weekends and Bank holidays. Now it is called Tortworth Visitors' Centre, which can be a little confusing as it is still a prison. It is well worth a call though. There is a good café, a first-class shop, a garden centre, and an Arts and Crafts Section.

The views are superb. On a clear day it is possible to see right over the Severn to the Forest of Dean. Perhaps only the Home Office could wangle for itself such a remarkable view as well as a prison.

The small hamlet with its nightmarish tree is within spitting distance. Satellite navigation is not required for a fascinating visit.

Uley

Many of the old names for Uley only arose through the Domesday Book.

These include Euuelege, Ewelegh and Huelega which move along to Euleg, Ule-Ley and Yewley.

These various names all give the same sound, and one school of thought is that they refer to a yew tree in a glade or clearing. Another group of historians insists that the name means ancient plants growing in a watering place.

What early people called the place we do not know, because Uley was popular long before the Romans. Archaeologists are fairly certain that people lived on top of the high ground more than 2,000 years before Christ.

One of the most spectacular Iron Age forts dominates the region, which shows how our ancestors appreciated the defensive benefits of high ground. Uley Bury had been calculated to be thirty-two acres, or thirteen hectares, in a rough rectangle.

Historians have worked out that 1,000 people lived at the fort. There would also be their animals, because domestic animals meant not just wealth but escape from starvation in the cold months.

What is strange, though, is that there is no water there today. These ancients could hardly have carried water up the stoop slopes for themselves and their animals. The local water table must have been much higher than it is today.

The fort had extensive defensive earthworks, which were enhanced by a steep slope upwards to where the people lived. It is thought there was terracing as well as an embankment. There was certainly an inner, as well as an outer, rampart.

Much of this region has been disturbed with the passage of so many centuries, but below the outer rampart there is a narrow outer terrace. This tells us that these people had given considerable thought to their defensive protection against animals, as well as invading man. It also shows that they had a pretty good grasp of military tactics.

Their homes would have been crude though they would have had to be capable of standing up to strong winds at the fort's elevation of 823 ft.

The people would have been meat-eaters and probably supplemented their diet with natural plants. Grain growing would have been tricky at that height. They would have had miserable lives in the cold, wet months of the year. The weak would have been whittled out in the first few years of life. Those that did survive the crucial first five years would have been tough although by the mid-twenties they would already have started suffering from rheumatism as a result of their wet homes.

A short distance from Uley Bury is Hetty Pegler's Tump. She was a local landowner and her name has stuck to the long, chambered barrow. It is thought that this too was probably built somewhere around 2900BC.

Excavations in the nineteenth century found at least fifteen human skeletons in the passages and chambers.

There are two chambers from a stone-built central passage with a small end one. This barrow was obviously of enormous importance to our ancestors.

The Romans came and went. So too, did the Normans. Gradually, the fort became of less importance and fell into disuse and disrepair. This did not mean that Uley sank into obscurity. Far from it. It became a village of huge importance.

In the seventeenth and eighteenth centuries there was much activity. It was John Eyles, in the seventeenth century, who was to become the first man to make the famous Spanish Cloth at Uley. This was sometimes also called Kerseymere.

It became famous as Uley Blue, a cloth much in demand for men's long-tailed coats. It certainly rivalled Stroud's famous red cloth.

Another famous man born at Eley in 1726 was Samuel Rudder, although the surname might have been changed from Rutter. He became a bookseller initially, and married Mary Hinton in 1749. He gradually went into book printing and his first venture was a Latin grammar work, which was advertised in 1752. His magnum opus was his famous *History of Gloucestershire* published in 1779 and still widely used. He died, aged eighty-four, in 1792.

From then on, for a number of years Uley trundled along in quite good times, all connected with the cloth industry, until 1833. Then the rot began. Trouble fell upon cloth manufacturing. This was brought about by far too much credit being handed out by Blackwell Hall, the head of the cloth industry. Too much money went on new-fangled machinery. A dozen out of nineteen manufacturers went out of production. This had a terrible effect upon the workers. In the county there were eighty-five bankruptcies. The cottage weavers fared particularly badly, because there was no other work. Many could not go to church because they had no clothing.

Often, they would all have to sleep on loose straw. Breakfast would normally be a little warm water flavoured with salt and pepper, accompanied by one crust of bread. There would be no midday meal, and supper would usually be bread, cheese or potatoes with a little hot fat poured over this mess.

The Poor Relief of many of the parishes simply could not cope with such a disaster. Far too many people were now out of work. There was only one thing for them to do – leave England, which they did.

Once started, a trickle became a flood and in 1837 more than 1,000 skilled workers, who had lost their jobs, emigrated to America or Australia.

Gradually, as the cloth industry declined all over the country so did little Uley slide back into rural tranquillity.

Today, though, the fort and tump remain for those who have strong climbing legs.

Uley itself is a delightful, peaceful village. Its appearance in 2000 gives no clue at all to its momentous history.

Wapley

Wapley and Codrington have always gone together like cheese and onions.

Wapley's old names were Wapelie or Wappelei while today's Codrington was simply Cotherington.

The old English word of wapol was usually taken to mean a pool or marsh though it can also mean plain bubbles. There are several springs in the hamlet of Wapley and the River Frome rises in the Codrington Hill to start its meandering trail to Bristol. Both of these little places lie in the Hundred of Grumbald's Ash and have never been significant.

An idea of a place's worth and size can usually be guessed at with the Domesday entry concerning slaves. There were just two which says it all.

It is interesting to note that a part of Wapley was considered a member of the great manor of Betune at one stage. Certainly it was royal land and written down as Terra Regis.

We know that the bishop of St Laud held Wapley in the Polscrecerce Hundred then an Alfred held it off him. This was during the reign of Edward.

During the early days there was a big row between the churches of the region. How it all started we do not know but it is certain that the Abbey of Stanleigh in Wiltshire crossed swords verbally with the Abbey of St Austins in Bristol.

It was all over a chapel. Stanleigh wanted to build a chapel at Codrington. St Austins objected very strongly. Their argument was that this would be most prejudicial to Wapley Church. They were the patrons of the latter, so they dug in the ecclesiastical toes.

This went on and on but was finally settled in 1280. Stanleigh came out the winner to a certain extent. They were given the go-ahead to build the chapel but only for local use. No one else had resort to it without the special permission from the minister at Wapley. So much for brotherly love in those days.

Some of the land in and around Codrington was, at one time, owned by a Benedictine Nunnery of Pynely, Warwickshire. This had been founded in the reign of Henry I by Robert de Pilardinton.

Religion was incredibly important all those centuries ago. Henry II gave both the manors of Wapley and Codrington to Radulf, son of a Stephen. He promptly gave them to the Abbey of Stanley. He had one object in mind for this gift. It was that they would pray for the soul of the king as well as that of the donor and his family.

We might call this hedging his bets today but it was a grave and serious matter then in ways we cannot really understand in the twenty-first century.

In the latter part of the thirteenth century there was more trouble in Wapley when the Writ of Quo Warranto was brought against the Abbott. It demanded he set forth his right to hold a court leet within the area. The Abbott then obtained a licence to alienate the manor of Wapley altogether but he craftily reserved a rent of £11 a year for the repair of his abbey so he did quite nicely.

Finally, it was all sold to John de Codrington and his heirs. Codrington obtained from Pope Martin V in the twelfth year of his pontificate, a licence for a portable altar so that mass could be consecrated wherever he pleased. Obviously another cautious individual where his soul was concerned.

One of the Codringtons fought with Henry V at the Battle of Agincourt and was the king's standard bearer. He is reputed to have lived to the incredible age of 111 years but this takes rather a lot of swallowing.

Gradually the manor passed away from the Codrington family through matrimony and was owned next by Sir Richard Bamfylde, a baronet though Codrington itself still retained connections with the more senior family.

Today, both Wapley and Codrington are small, insignificant places where nothing appears to happen. Wapley is perhaps the smaller of the two. In 1712 there were just forty-five houses with only 180 inhabitants. Of these only five were freeholders. Now it is off the beaten track, just about forgotten even though it is so near to bustling Yate.

At the top of a hill runs the B4465. Just up from the hill's crossroads, on one side, starts an unusual bridle path for riders and hikers. The easiest way to find this is to look for a mass of hoof prints. This really is a very minor road but the Council have blocked access to all vehicles leaving this delightful bridle path for the riders and hikers.

Because of this, Nature runs riot and along this path can be found flora and fauna, which have long vanished from chemical-laden areas. At this point it is known on local maps as Burbarrow Lane and it is a little gem to explore. From this lane other bridle paths, though shorter ones, branch off to right and left. Then the explorer crosses the M4 motorway via a purpose-built bridge. Once again the council have fixed vehicular obstructions so a huge variety of wild flowers can be found. In one place there is even a Rose of Sharon which can only have been planted with the compliments of the birds.

Heading down a stony section the lane's name changes to Wash Pool Lane. There is a ford to cross, which can run quite deep after heavy rain and there is no footpath at all so hikers be warned. Some horses also object to wet hooves so a tight seat in the saddle is necessary.

The Lane ends slap bang in the yard of the Ring of Bells Farm near to Hinton Common. If a person turns left and travels for a short distance there is a continuation which comes out on the Doynton Lane. Before this though a bridle path extends on the right which goes up a fairly steep hill and comes out on Rookery Lane. At a few points now, with the right weather conditions, it becomes possible to see parts of the Severn Valley. Indeed at one angle of the B4465 the Severn Bridges are visible.

These old bridle paths, especially when not fouled by vehicles, give a beautiful picture of old Gloucestershire as it has been for centuries. There is sometimes a modern farming aspect, which does not go amiss, when the farmers plant both Flax and Rape – one bright yellow and the other a delicate blue. Combined with the natural greenery these colours must ensure a kaleidoscope of colour from the air.

Places like Burbarrow Lane, the ford and Wash Pool Lane are to be treasured because they give us an England which has so often vanished elsewhere. They might also be considered uniquely Gloucestershire.

Westerleigh

Westerleigh has had the usual variety of old-fashioned names. Two of these are Westerlega and Westarleygh. A rough translation tells us this means a westerly glade or clearing.

The village is not mentioned in the Domesday Book, because it came under the thumb of the powerful and large Pucklechurch hundred. It was considered a mere offshoot.

It was given to the monks of Glastonbury and they were expected to pray for the soul of the murdered King Edmund. After a time, though, they gave the village away on the strict condition that Joceline, the Bishop of Bath and Wells, would allow them to elect their own abbot. Even monks in those days could develop a bolshie streak when it suited their purposes. They usually managed to get their own way as they did in this case.

Many incomers to Yate look upon Westerleigh as nothing but a vague suburb of their town. It is anything but, though. Indignant village residents hasten to point out a few confirmed facts of life.

They are separated from big sister Yate by a few fields, a railway line and bridge and some other facts. For those in the historical know, there is the very interesting point that for many decades, even a couple of centuries, Westerleigh had a much larger population than that of Yate. The records show that in 1801 Westerleigh had 1,582 inhabitants. All Yate could boast was 654. Why the difference? It was the old story – coal.

This was the industry which provided the valuable work for the men and boys. A report of the State of the Westerleigh Coal in 1792 mentions a Serridge engine – obviously of very great importance.

In the next fifty years the Ram Hill Pit was sunk, then that for the New Engine Pit. Both of these were linked underground to Churchlease and the Rose Oak Pits. They were later sited on the middle branch of the Bristol and Gloucester Railway.

The oval shaft of Ram Hill was said to be 558 feet deep and was originally worked by a horse gin. It seems likely these enterprises were not profitable because Westerleigh Pit was abandoned in the late 1860s.

Another cottage industry aped that of Pucklechurch – felt

hats were made. This was a highly dangerous occupation for all workers because of the brain damage from the chemicals.

Like so many South Gloucestershire villages, Westerleigh was owned by many people until it finally came into the hands of the Poyntz family.

Afterwards, John Roberts, a Bristol alderman, bought it and became lord of the manor in 1608. He was a very generous man to those less fortunate than himself in life. He gave the church house and a cottage called Buy Hays to feoffees for the benefit of the poor. This was like putting something in trust for the use of a third party.

Another generous resident was Edward Hill who died in 1619. He left the huge sum of £100, which was laid out on land to yield an annual income of £14.

Of this sum £3.50 was to be given to the poor on Candlemass Day. This was around 2nd February. On this day all candles were blessed. Candles were vital to the people's lives, far more important than we can hope to understand. The residue of his money went to help apprentices of the parish who came from poor families.

One other important person born in the village was Doctor Edward Fowler. He rose to become Bishop of Gloucester.

Two other wealthy and generous men were Robert Nailer and Sir John Smyth. The former paid for a boy's apprenticeship and the latter left enough money to ensure poor children could be taught to read and write. In those days education was of enormous importance. It was the only way in which the poor could hope to elevate themselves and their children. The ability to read and write was treasured more than gold.

That the village is very old can be confirmed by one particular building; Ye Olde Inne, which stands cheek by jowl with the church. It is quite fascinating, not only in its construction and design, but in its proven history.

In was constructed as long ago as 1270, which must make it one of the very oldest buildings anywhere near to Yate. Its original name was the King's Arms and there is even a possibility there was a prior building just for drinking purposes.

It is a rare discovery to learn this inn was there before the church. While the church was being built by monks, they lived at the King's Arms. History does not relate how much nor how often they were happy to imbibe.

The building oozes olde world charm. Under the floor of what is called the smallest bar in the country, there was a cellar with the well. There were also passages that led to the church in one direction and the priory in the other.

These are not accessible now at all. The floor of the smallest bar has been covered over with ancient flagstones.

In this small front bar there is a highly unusual window. It has been decorated with leaves from the Westonbirt Arboretum. On the top right-hand window there is a very sad, poignant reminder of World War II. In the Walloon language a refugee painstakingly scratched the following:

> Here I spoke. Here I Drank,
> In the Company of Friends,
> During the Nazi Occupation of my Homeland
> between 1941 and 1945.

The licensee, John King has met the son of the man who wrote this heartbreaking, wistful message and also a grandchild.

In what is known as the Pit Bar the licensee recently removed a modern fireplace. Underneath he discovered a very old-fashioned one, capable of holding a small spit, and it is thought this was the original one used to cook the monks' food while they built the church.

Between the bars and the passageway there is a highly unusual collection of Westerleigh memorabilia, which includes an authentic road sign. These photographs show the village as it was decades ago.

There is another highly unusual historical connection with

the USA. A Mr Crandle, when a baby, was baptised at the church next door. When adult he went to America and settled south of Boston. He founded a village which he proudly called Westerley.

During the last few years the licensee has extended the inn and successfully retained its ancient charm. There is a stunning conservatory in which meals are taken. The food served is genuine olde English. It is all fresh with the most imaginative desserts, delightful enough to spur on the most jaded pudding appetite.

The inn's food speciality is also fish, particularly Dover soles. There is nothing frozen or mundane. Junk food is not allowed past the front door.

The licensee runs a tight ship, but one in which all are made genuinely welcome and can feel perfectly at ease as if at home. All this natural charm is complemented by the history of the building itself.

Ye Olde Inne is Westerleigh, the whole enveloped by the history of our country.

Wickwar

When people drive through the main street of Wickwar, the wags look around, see no one, and say the place is a ghost town. It was not always so – far from it.

Even in Domesday, it was home to nine villagers, fourteen smallholders and five slaves. This was quite a population for a small place, especially the number of slaves.

Wickwar has had the usual variety of names before its present one. These range from Wichen and Whictenua to Warre Wyke. The Olde English Wicum means 'at the dwellings' while the 'war' portion comes from an ancient Norman de la Warre family.

John la Warre came over with William the Conqueror and was given the manor. This was confirmed by King John and afterwards fell to his heirs. It was held with the simple 'tax' of but one knight – a very cheap form of payment at those times.

John's son, called Jordan, must have been the usual rebellious youth. He often joined with others in spats against both King John and Henry III, though it is not at all clear exactly what he hoped to gain.

Another son of this family purchased rights to a market which used to be held on Tuesdays. There was also a yearly fair on Whit Monday plus the two following days. This tells us that Wickwar then was certainly no ghost town. It was a very thriving, busy commercial town. Edward I certainly thought so because he granted the market and fair.

In the reign of Edward III another la Warre stood in high prominence – Roger la Warre attended the king on his wars in France and he was present at the battle of Poitiers in 1356. At this battle, the French king, his son and other nobles were taken prisoner. All this made very good commercial business. The higher the rank of the person captured, the greater the ransom which could be demanded for their release. War in those days was as much commercial as martial. For his share in this exploit Roger also had a 'campet' or 'chape' of that monarch's sword assigned to him. Afterwards he and his family always used this on their armorial bearings.

For a while after this there is the normal line of male descent, then the estate passes to the family of Thomas West. There was an entail on the property, quite normal for those times. The estate came to the Wests through the marriage of Joan, daughter of the last Warre, into the West family. Wickwar was now a bustling town indeed and it was called Wyke-Warr after the great Warre family.

Then we come to a little mayhem. A William West, son of Sir George West, was brought up in the manor by his uncle, Thomas de la Warr. It is obvious William considered himself the natural heir but he must have been of an impatient nature.

He preferred not to await normal events and tried to poison his uncle to hurry things along a little.

He did not succeed and a strong complaint was made in Parliament. William became damned. He could not succeed his uncle now and his allowance was cut down to £350 a year – a paltry sum for one used to living with wealth. At least though he had managed to keep his head attached to his neck.

As he started to mature good showed in him though. He must have realised he had been dealt with very lightly by Parliament. He joined the English army at the siege of St Quintin in 1557. He carried himself very well under arms for a longish period – so well, he was given a knighthood at Hampton Court in 1568. He was also given a new title, Lord de la Warr. By another Act of Parliament, he received full restitution in blood rights and so, at last, he received the manor that he had craved when young and foolish.

After his death he left a son, Thomas, and this man also had mettle. He became the Captain General of the plantations in Virginia, sailing there in three small ships in 1609. While in the New World he explored and made many important discoveries. Unfortunately his health suffered and he died on a voyage back to England. All round, they were an enterprising family of the warrior blood, even if some had tried to jump the gun or changed sides in royal disputes rather too easily.

Wickwar had had other famous sons too. A boy by the name of Alexander Hosea was obviously a person of considerable spirit – he ran away from home and went to London. During many years there he became a very rich man, though history does not give us the hows or whys. He never forgot Wickwar though, and in his will, dated 1683, he left the means for a school to be founded there. By 1894 the establishment became an elementary school. A provision was made for there to be an exhibition (scholarship) to a higher school with a grant of £30 – quite a handsome sum.

Another great son of Wickwar was William Russell of Lincoln

College, Oxford. At one time he was a schoolmaster at Chipping Sodbury School. He was well-known for a broadside against John Biddle, the Socinian, with his book *Blasphemoklonian – The Holy Ghost Vindicated.* He too seems to have been another strong Wickwar character.

At one time the town had its own mayor and corporation, and there were four malt houses and two breweries. Gradually, though, like so many small places, it fell into a gentle decline. Before it reached its 'ghost town' status, it had one more burst of glory, which put even mighty Bristol to shame – one of the breweries had its own small streets lit with electricity.

About the year 1890, a chemist named Ansell, was employed at one of the breweries. He was deeply interested in electricity and installed the system in his workplace. The lamps were of the carbon arc types – what our great-grandparents might have seen in old 'magic lantern' shows. The brewery owner was so delighted with the results he had the power line, carrying some fifty volts, extended to his home at the other end of the street from his brewery.

In 1894, when the parish council came into being, it decided to tap these wires. By doing this, they were able to install electric lighting using the same current. Instead of the normal oil lamps common in homes of that time, Wickwar blazed at night with electricity. This was long before Bristol worked around to doing this. Wickwar was rather smug about all this – with justification.

In the last century Wickwar sank back to being a quiet little village and now, in the twenty-first century, it is the same. It still has a brewery but most of the rest of its old businesses have gone except a trading estate. It has new houses, a good gardening centre, and all around, delightful Cotswold views.

If it is a ghost town, surely those ghosts are the warriors of old?

Winterbourne

Winterbourne had two earlier versions of its name, Winterbourne and Winterburn. It means a stream which runs chiefly in the winter rains.

At Bury Hill an ancient camp which covered seven and a half acres has been discovered. It is reasonable to assume the ramparts were erected by the Celts. Naturally the Romans would be delighted to come across this.

They made a line of forts all along the high ground that faced the Severn and, more importantly, the Silures tribe of South Wales, Bury Hill camp was made to link this line of forts and some of the Romans' Cotswold camps.

A Roman army hut was also discovered, enclosed by a four-foot ditch. Remains of a wall were also found but this was only about one foot tall.

This suggests the rest of the walls were only of timber and sod. Once raised, the roof would be of brushwood – not an elaborate affair by Roman standards. It tells us this was probably nothing but a frontier outpost initially and probably made during the AD47 campaign.

During the third and fourth centuries it is certain the Romans were present on a more permanent basis because of the artefacts which have been found – coins and glass fragments of the period.

Winterbourne was part and parcel of the great Royal Forest of Kingswood during the later reigns of the Saxon kings. This went on right after the Conquest until 1228 when Henry III issued his charter of deforestation. After this, much of the land was cleared and converted to common land. Only a small portion was retained as a Royal Chase.

The Saxons divided the land into tithings. Each one was considered adequate to maintain ten households. Ten tithings formed a Hundred. Winterbourne was in the Hundred of Langley and Swineshead.

Domesday changed everything to shires, putting in place a tenant in chief under the feudal system. In reality it meant it all belonged to the lord of the manor, held for the king. Under Edward the Confessor, this was Aluin, although it seems to have been firmly kept in royal hands afterwards until the reign of Henry II.

For a long time after Aluin, the region was held by Reginald de Cahoine and Ralph Fitzstephen. Other lords held parts, sometimes not always successfully.

In 1320 Sir John Giffard held a moiety of the manor and seized Robert de Hadele unjustly. It all becomes a bit tangled now but Giffard would not release him until he had made a claim of the tenancy.

Not that Giffard did very well afterwards. He took part in the conspiracy against Edward II, which led to execution. His castle at Brimpsfield was razed.

Gradually the manor went into the ownership of the Bradestons. Thomas, Lord Berkeley, and the Sheriff, told Bardeston to pick 200 archers to fight France. Some of these would certainly have come from Winterbourne. In the Calais Roll it states Bradeston fought in the King's Division at the Battle of Crecy. He only visited Winterbourne now and again, probably to collect rents and dues.

The Bucks family then had the manor and elected to fight for the Royalists in the Civil Wars. They had made a bad choice. Bucks was fined exceptionally heavily by Parliament, which ruined him.

For quite a while the manor was then held by the Smyth family of Long Ashton but eventually they too sold it on. It became the custom of these lords of the manor to grant leases for ninety-nine years or three lives.

In 1780 the Whalley family, who owned the manor, granted the lease of a cottage to Thomas Mauler for ninety-nine years.

The yearly rent was two good, fat pullets and a Heriot, or insurance, of 6s 8d on the death of each of three nominees on the lease.

In the eighteenth century Winterbourne's speciality was making beaver hats. These small cottage industries failed with the introduction of cheap silk hats from France. At the same time, beaver pelts had risen in price.

We know that in 1393 the rights of a market and two fairs were granted to be held yearly for the lady of the manor, Blanche Bradeston. It is thought the market may have been held somewhere near the parish church. The two fairs took place on a space before the George and Dragon. They seem to have stopped by 1870, probably through lack of attendance.

In the late eighteenth century, William Pitt became alarmed at France's military expansion and the Winterbourne Troop came into being with William Perry as Captain.

A local man named Higgins, the son of a farmer, with his brother, became a notorious highwayman. He was caught, convicted and shipped to America. He promptly escaped, robbed a house for his passage money and, within three months, was back in the district. One of his brothers was then hanged which sobered him temporarily. He changed his name to Hickson and went to live in Clifton but robbed a train, was caught and went to trial. He was finally sentenced to be hanged.

Winterbourne slumped back into rural quiet until houses started to appear as the villages near Bristol acquired popularity. With the growth of industry at Patchway and Filton, plus the great god the motor car, Winterbourne can often turn into a hideous, road-rage-inducing nightmare – not the clean tranquil place it was centuries ago.

Wotton-Under-Edge

This little town's name has an olde worlde charm but the first varieties are harsh to our ears. They range from Aet Wude and Wudutune to the more simple Vutune and Wutton which we are able to recognise. An affix usually means a farmstead in the wood as well as under the Cotswold escarpment. In total, the town had eighteen old names, some of which were real tongue twisters.

It was in the Dudstone Hundred though it is also mentioned in a land grant of 940. It all belonged to William Breakwolf who held it directly from the king. Domesday says there were two ploughs, four smallholders and four slaves. A little insignificant place, certainly not worthy of the word town.

Early Wotton was, like too many other Gloucestershire habitations, heavily tied in with the Berkeley family because they became the owners of the region's manor.

Wotton has not always been exactly tranquil either. It has had its moments of notoriety and never more so than in the thirteenth century. King John had many mercenaries fighting for him and these men, like all of their breed, were of a very decided and uncertain temperament. They only went to war for what they could get out of the fighting. Dying was merely a secondary occupation to them.

For some reason, they took it into their heads to burn Wotton down. It is most likely they were aided and abetted by their royal paymaster because John had the typical erratic Angevin temper. Nothing which concerned this family can really cause surprise.

Once anyone ruffled John's feathers – quite simple to do at any time – his mood and temper would always change for the worst. It certainly would not have taken any great effort to destroy Wotton either.

Most of the houses would have been constructed from wood and with a stiff wind there would have been little the inhabitants could do except curse the king but very discreetly.

However, the townspeople came from rugged stock and they were not going to be put off their stride by a dubious monarch. They promptly set to and rebuilt their homes. In doing this, they decided to concentrate upon plots of a third of an acre. Many of these can still be worked out today on a grid of the old town, especially towards the south.

The church was erected in 1283 and in the fourteenth century, a tower was added with a splendid example of the perpendicular style of building, inside of which were put many fine brasses over the years, most of which were connected with the Berkeley family.

These include Thomas who fought at Agincourt and his wife, the Lady Margaret. She is shown wearing a long cloak with a little dog at her feet. An organ was installed later on, which it is reputed the great composer Handel played when on a visit.

Another famous Berkeley heavily connected with Wotton was Katherine, Lady Berkeley. She was a lady of very great wealth who did not have one greedy or selfish hair on her head. She inherited enormous riches from her first husband, Sir Peter de Veel of Charfield. Then she became the wife of Thomas III, Lord Berkeley in 1347.

It was Lady Katherine who founded the school that bears her name to this day, and which is justifiably proud to declare it is the oldest operating school in the country. In our modern times, the school is now situated just outside the town and is extremely proud and famous for its superb languages' department.

For many years Wotton was famous for its cloth-making which provided work for many. The steep hills gave the necessary running water for the fulling and rows of simple cottages were constructed for the weavers. During the nineteenth century, there was an insidious change which had devastating effects upon the workers.

The mill owners started to turn their backs upon cloth-making.

Instead they opted to invest their monies in land and grand houses. At the same time, their sons were encouraged to enter the professions rather than to stay in trade. This was the day and age when the upper classes were inclined to look down their snooty noses at any man or family connected with trade. It often ruined the potential marriage prospects of many a fine young lady. Trade carried no cachet.

There were other generous patrons of the town so three sets of almshouses were built for the poor and needy. There is the Rowland Hill rank connected to what was formerly the Tabernacle Church, another set going out of town on the Coombe Road and the third in Church Street. These latter may be considered the most attractive. They are only a handful in number but they boast a tiny courtyard, which members of the public can explore, plus a diminutive chapel. This tiny building has an air of enormous peace and repose. There are two small stained glass windows over the altar, which are quite charming. There is also a visitors' book and a study of this shows people visit from all over the world. Without exception, all are entranced with this chapel's tranquillity.

Sir Isaac Pitman of shorthand fame, lived and taught here for a few years before being sacked from his position for his downright radical views. He then went to work and live in Bath. He was strong-minded enough to object to school governors and church wardens in their attempts to dictate his thoughts.

Tolstoy House once held the Court of Piepowder. This name is a corruption of the French and loosely translates to 'dusty feet'. It meant that poor people, who walked everywhere and arrived with their dusty feet, could put their case forward in this court to receive justice.

A number of the buildings incorporate bits and pieces of rubble and masonry from one of the Shire's last medieval foundations at nearby Kingswood.

This building was barely completed before the Monasteries were all dissolved and their assets sold off. Much of the masonry was eagerly seized upon by the residents of Wotton for use in their private constructions.

One of the greatest grabbers of all was Sir Nicholas Poyntz. He hastily took away whatever he could manage to carry for building a new hunting lodge near to Alderney. Somehow though, the gatehouse managed to survive against all this blatant thieving and has now been restored.

All of this town's architecture is worth studying to pick out the various styles There are some superb old buildings, a few of which have unusual windows. One is Tolstoy House, built in the seventeenth century as a country house plus courtroom. In the town centre, more buildings huddle up together, all worth a steady scrutiny instead of a cursory glance.

Wotton and the surrounding area is very popular with hikers who walk the Cotswold Way because this well-known trail actually comes through the town centre.

From nearly every angle in the town, there are views which delight the eye and a full exploration may be obtained from the excellent Heritage Centre at The Chippings, near the main car park.

Parking the car is the usual small town's nightmare but well worth the hassle involved. For the visitor who wishes to see something just a little bit out of the ordinary, Wotton-under-Edge has a lot to offer. Go and find out for yourself.

Yate

Yate has its share of delightful gems for those who take the trouble to explore and find them.

Possibly one of the prettiest is Yate Rocks, barely two miles from the town as the crow flies The lane is rather narrow and hardly suitable for cars, but there is a sprinkling of charming houses, most of which have delightful views over our part of the county on a good day.

At the bottom of the hill is an ancient ford. In summer this is usually nothing but dried gravel. In winter, though, it can change to a bustling rush of water.

This is one of the tributaries of Ladden Brook, a small waterway that meanders in all directions through the fields, as if totally confused as to which direction it should really flow. It takes a long time to make up its mind before it finally joins the River Frome at Cogsmill near Iron Acton and loses its own identity completely.

Yate Rocks has retained an almost chocolate-box beauty reminiscent of what our land used to be like before the modern march of time. The hedges and fields make natural wildlife homes, virtually undisturbed by intruding man.

Not far away, roughly a mile north, is a house which bristles with history just about impossible to prove. In fact, it was built by Mr Oxwich, who was lord of the manor in the seventeenth century. Records often dub him Oxwick, so take your pick.

He is somewhat a man of mystery. After the civil wars, Yate Court was left a total ruin and Oxwick bought it with the idea of rebuilding. This was rather a grandiose scheme, because the Parliamentarians' cannons had done a very thorough job of total destruction.

Somewhat annoyed, Oxwick gave up this idea and decided to build his own house instead. The result was Oxwick Hall, which is privately owned today. It has a slight Cotswold style, with steep gables. The lines of elevation are possibly more vertical than horizontal. There are red brick jambs and arches to the doors. It is certainly eye-catching but whether one considers it delightful or not depends upon architectural taste.

Oxwick was a mysterious character. There are two stories about him, neither of which are capable of being proven at this distance of time. That Oxwick was rich is not disputed, but from where he obtained this wealth is the bone of contention.

One dogmatic school of thought says he was a London

fishmonger and a member of the Fishmongers' Company of London.

There might be a grain of truth in this, but the second story is perhaps more plausible – that his ill-gotten gains came from slaving. He was a dealer in the miseries of human flesh. As Bristol was such an important slaving centre, many believe this is the truer account. It does have the ring of feasibility.

Little is known of his character, except he must have had more than a streak of bloody-mindedness in him. Oxwick and the vicar of the day could not stand each other. The clashes between the lord of the manor and Christ's representative were awesome and well-known.

William Mason, the rector, reciprocated in full. What started it all off, we have no idea. Oxwick's wealth, if it did indeed come from slaving, might have been the trigger. Perhaps though, it was a simple case of two human beings who took an instant dislike to each other.

Matters progressed in a dramatic fashion. The two strong-minded, rather difficult men, entered into a long-standing legal dispute over church tithes.

Mason was rather good at this because, in 1691, a local by the name of Robert Neale went to prison for refusing to pay these tithes. In the years following, wheat was taken from his fields in lieu of the tithes, even if it meant lifting a locked gate off its hinges.

So if Oxwick decided he too would refuse to pay, Mason simply followed his instincts. He went to law. It was a suit which dragged on for years, as was normal in those times. The vicar eventually won, though at what cost is debatable.

It is known that Oxwick dabbled in land speculation, but whether it was the lord of the manor himself or a son is unknown. Possibly it was Oxwick senior, who then rather burned his fingers over Yate Court's ruins.

It is thought that Oxwick Hall was built somewhere around 1702. A worn plaque gives a date, which might also read 1722.

Around this time, Yate had only eighty houses with roughly 320 inhabitants, so it was a mediocre little place compared to Chipping Sodbury, its dominant big brother.

Another oddball character was a very old Quaker gentleman who lived in Yate proper at the house known as Yate Lawn. This house was also gabled and its owner was Tobias Sturge, known commonly and very popularly as plain Toby.

Toby was a Quaker by religion but also had an awkward streak. He too objected to paying tithes. This rebellious act against the church seems to have been commonplace.

Those who could object, did – much as we would all like to give a certain gesture to the Inland Revenue today. Toby decided he was not going to pay, come hell or high water.

Instead, he very cleverly avoided a lawsuit with a cunning play. He allowed sheep, to the value of the sum demanded, to be taken from his flock instead of money, so honour was satisfied all round.

Another delightful gem is Poole Court, once a superb family home, built in the mid-nineteenth century. A map of 1842 gives the site of today's Poole Court as that of a property labelled simply as Poole House Farm.

Surrounding the farmhouse were fields, with the church standing slightly north and the Lion Inn east. There was a huge pond on the site of today's Morrison's roundabout. The house stood back from the main road – now Station Road, but then The Turnpike to Bristol.

Poole Court's owner was Richard Hill of shipping fame and his home had a very chequered history. George Parnall bought it in 1925 after its World War One use as an officers' mess for the Flying Corps. It changed hands again in 1932, and came into the possession of the Newman family. As their business expanded, the house became offices.

By 1988 though, Newman's whole site was acquired by property developers and threats were being muttered that Poole Court was to be demolished to make way for more housing. Yate Town council sprang into action. After much convoluted talking, plus more than a few disagreements, the council finally bought it from the property developers, for the enormous sum of exactly one pound.

It then had the foresight to restore the building to its old splendour. The idea was that Poole Court would belong to the people of Yate for their use. In 1990, the building was opened after a £1.5 million facelift. The formal ceremony was performed by the Burgermeister of Yate's twin town of Bad Salzdetfurth in Germany.

Today this wonderful building is available for all. It houses the town council. It performs weddings. There are rooms for community group meetings, a function suite for parties and wedding receptions and business seminars and now, not far away, the new heritage centre. It is a truly remarkable building and it belongs to the people of Yate. Incredible value for £1!

These gems are all around Yate, for those who have the nowse to explore and find them.

To many people, today's Yate is a brash, new, upstart town dominated by the shopping centre but Yate has had its days of glory. It has also known some weird characters who did not give a damn about convention either.

Long before the conquest, Yate had its own monastery. Today we think of this purely as a religious house but in those distant times a monastery was also a vibrant trading house. Perhaps some might consider it was a forerunner of Tesco!

Where this monastery was sited is something about which it appears the academic historians do not agree. It must have been near to the north-south track leading to the higher land above today's Chipping Sodbury. Very little else is known, though perhaps one day the earth might yield valuable clues.

The most important building was Yate Court which also had its deer park.

The great family were the Berkeleys, though how long they lived depended upon where they stood in favour with the king of that time.

Perhaps one of the greatest characters to live at the Court was Lady Anne, widow of Thomas, Lord Berkeley who died in 1534. She had great troubles with her late husband's brother, Maurice, who had avaricious eyes on the title and estates.

However, Maurice was exceedingly premature in his thieving attempts, because Lady Anne gave birth to Lord Berkeley's posthumous son. Now Maurice was completely foiled but he decided instead to make Lady Anne's life exceedingly difficult. She was a lady of considerable spirit who did not really give a damn for anyone. Perhaps also Lady Anne had done her best to make Maurice's life a misery by trying to dispossess him in turn.

One night Maurice decided to burn her out of house and home. Unfortunately for the men he sent for this task, some other men had decided it was an ideal time to do a little Yate poaching in the deer park. Each group ran into the other in the dark and both sides frightened themselves to death. Lord Maurice's men thought the poachers were Lady Anne's men and promptly fled the scene. The poachers, with considerable foresight, told Lady Anne and, by doing so, saved their own skins.

Lady Anne was outraged and promptly instigated an action against Maurice in the notorious Star Chamber in which he was lucky enough to get away with heavy fines.

Another time Lady Anne lost her temper when the religious complained about her servants playing tennis on a Sunday. She spat back at them that she would 'sit upon their skyrtes!' Her son, Henry, and daughter Elizabeth were wild and feckless but much loved by the locals who had always adored a 'character'. Lord Henry married Catherine Howard when he was only twenty and during the first four years of this marriage lived far beyond his means.

Probably the most famous time for Yate Court though was during the Civil Wars. The court was held by Parliament but it was isolated in a sea of Royalists. It was obvious they would soon be forced to surrender so Colonel Massey came to their rescue with 300 dragoons.

The Royalists were at Chipping Sodbury in force so that was their first move. Luckily for them, the Royalist sentry bolted at their approach and the rest of the Royalists followed quickly. It was a sweeping victory for Massey.

He took all the villagers' carts and marched to the court to relieve the isolated Roundheads and their depleted stores. These were sent off on pack trains while the canons were removed from the court. The villagers' carts, no longer needed, were carefully placed in the deer park undamaged and were collected by the villagers the next day. Then Massey gave the order and the canon pounded Yate Court into smithereens. It could never be used by the Royalists but a wonderful piece of Yate history had gone for ever.

Mr Oxwick, Lord of the Manor, bought the ruins with grandiose ideas of rebuilding the shattered court but it was a hopeless task. Perhaps also the fact that he appeared to be in constant, violent dispute with the vicar of Yate Church might have had something to do with this.

Certainly Yate Court was never touched again, and today the scene is ruled over by the animals, birds and plants of the wild. All that remains is the gateway, which was removed to Berkeley Castle.

Yate also had its glory days with coal mining when pits proliferated, including that down Eggshill Lane. Pubs go hand in glove with pits because mining is thirsty work. At one time, before the 1914-18 war, Yate's pubs and pits almost rivalled anything that could have been found in South Yorkshire.

It's all gone now but the history remains. Yate is not really a 'new' town. Its roots go back into antiquity so when you drive around the new estates and recent developments, do not be fooled into thinking Yate is brashly new. Deep down, it is 'old hat'.